Tim Huxley

Disintegrating Indonesia? Implications for Regional Security

Adelphi Paper 349

Oxford University Press, Great Clarendon Street, Oxford OX2 6DP
Oxford New York
Athens Auckland Bangkok Bombay Calcutta Cape Town
Dar es Salaam Delhi Florence Hong Kong Istanbul Karachi
Kuala Lumpur Madras Madrid Melbourne Mexico City
Nairobi Paris Singapore Taipei Tokyo Toronto
and associated companies in
Berlin Ibadan

Oxford is a trade mark of Oxford University Press

Published in the United States
by Oxford University Press Inc., New York

First published July 2002 by **Oxford University Press** for
The International Institute for Strategic Studies
Arundel House, 13–15 Arundel Street, Temple Place, London WC2R 3DX
www.iiss.org

Director John Chipman
Editor Mats Berdal
Assistant Editor Matthew Foley
Production Shirley Nicholls

British Library Cataloguing in Publication Data
Data available

Library of Congress Cataloguing in Publication Data

ISBN 0-19-851668-1
ISSN 0567-932x

Contents

Maps and tables

Introduction

Indonesia is South-east Asia's most populous and geographically extensive state. It is also the world's largest Muslim country. Although under its first president, Sukarno, the country was a major source of insecurity during the first half of the 1960s, between the late 1960s and the late 1990s regional and Western governments alike felt able to take for granted its domestic political stability, predictable regional foreign policy and generally pro-Western orientation. However, since the ousting of President Suharto in 1998 and the subsequent outbreak of violence in many parts of the archipelago, there has been much speculation in South-east Asia and the West over whether Indonesia has a future as a coherent nation-state. The security implications of disintegration would clearly be huge.

The key characteristic of Suharto's New Order regime, which seized power in 1965, was the prioritisation of economic development and national cohesion over political freedom. Although Indonesia had tentative pre-colonial antecedents, its modern territorial form was only established under Dutch colonial rule, which stretched from the late sixteenth to the early twentieth century. Indonesia is a huge country, composed of approximately 13,000 islands. Its population of more than 200 million means that it is the world's fourth most populous state. It is extraordinarily diverse in ethnic, linguistic and religious terms. Officially, almost 90% of its people adhere to Islam. However, beliefs and traditions deriving from Hinduism, Buddhism and animism have traditionally

Map 1 Indonesia and its regional setting

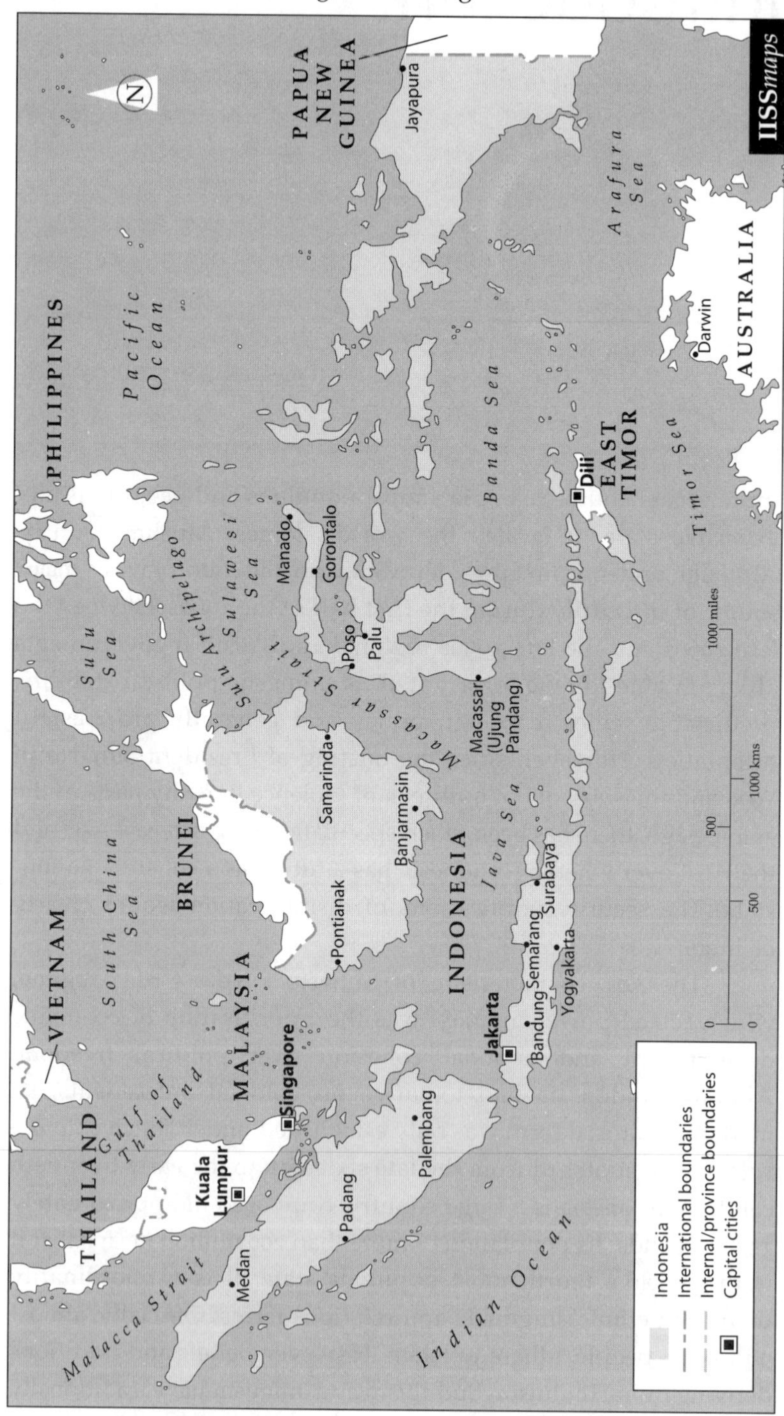

diluted the Islamic practices of many Indonesians. A sizeable Christian minority is concentrated in eastern Indonesia, Bali's population is largely Hindu and an ethnic Chinese minority, though amounting to no more than a few per cent of the total population, controls a large part of the economy.

Although Indonesia's population is preponderantly Muslim, the military-dominated New Order enforced a sense of national unity through the state philosophy of Pancasila, which emphasises religious tolerance. Despite the national motto of 'Unity in Diversity', however, there were serious tensions beneath the surface of Suharto's Indonesia. The New Order ran the country as a rigorously centralised empire, in which the provinces lacked significant economic – let alone political – autonomy. Although civilian technocrats played important parts in the government, under the system of *dwi fungsi* (dual function) the armed forces dominated at both national and local levels, providing cabinet ministers, provincial governors and district heads. There were growing pressures from resource-rich regions for a fairer distribution of national wealth, and the government in Jakarta faced armed struggles by provincial independence movements in Irian Jaya (now Papua) and Aceh. In East Timor, a former Portuguese colony invaded and occupied by Indonesia in 1975, a larger-scale resistance struggle attracted international sympathy. By the 1990s, there was also more generalised agitation for greater political freedom. Huge social and economic inequities persisted. Government corruption was endemic, starting with the president and his family.

The regional economic crisis in 1997–98 dramatically reinforced pressure for political change. Following Suharto's loss of support from the political and military establishment, the installation in May 1998 of an interim administration led by B. J. Habibie opened the way for democratic parliamentary elections in June 1999, and for the appointment of a new president, Abdurrahman Wahid, the following October. However, Abdurrahman proved incapable of managing his coalition government effectively and, harried by the still-influential armed forces as well as by his political opponents, he only survived as president until July 2001, when parliament replaced him with his vice-president, Megawati Sukarnoputri.

Four years after Suharto was forced to step down, Indonesia's democratisation remains incomplete. Party politics has been revived, but there is little respect for the rule of law: the rich and powerful figures guilty of large-scale corruption have mainly escaped justice. Security-sector reform has a long way to go, and the military is still an important power-broker. Civilian political control of the armed forces remains nominal: military elements still operate with substantial autonomy and impunity. Senior military officers bearing command responsibility for gross human-rights violations were only beginning to face trial in 2002. The police remain unable to assume internal-security duties.

The lack of effective security-sector reform has exacerbated the violence plaguing Indonesia's outer provinces. As well as initiating a democratic transition, Suharto's downfall allowed a major policy change with regard to East Timor, leading indirectly but rapidly to the territory's freedom from Indonesia. Although this successful separation encouraged secessionism in Aceh and Papua, the government in Jakarta will not allow these rebellious provinces more than a form of autonomy that permits a large measure of self-government and substantially greater provincial benefit from the exploitation of local resources. Less extensive autonomy has been granted to other regions as a means of pre-empting secessionist tendencies. At the same time, however, Megawati's administration has allowed the military to pursue a repressive 'security solution' against separatist movements in Aceh and Papua, despite clear evidence that such an approach has proved counter-productive in the past.

While there is no prospect that the two main separatist conflicts will be subdued in the foreseeable future, there seems little likelihood that Indonesia will disintegrate in the short term. However, an array of factors, including the impact of internal migration and the side-effects of administrative and fiscal autonomy, has stimulated communal tensions in many parts of Indonesia, often between Muslims and Christians. In some provinces, notably Maluku, Central Sulawesi and Kalimantan, these tensions have resulted in chronic violence, such that parts of the country have sometimes slipped out of central-government control.

At the same time, tension between Islamic and secular political forces has grown in Java, where many political organisations possess paramilitary wings. Although most Indonesian Muslims remain politically moderate and of a secular-nationalist disposition, extremist Islamic groups have proliferated since 1998, drawing strength from the removal of political restraints, widespread poverty, growing anti-Westernism and, in some cases, sponsorship from disgruntled military officers. While demands for the imposition of *sharia* law will not succeed while Megawati is president, the next elections, in 2004, could produce a more accommodating political environment. Any serious challenge to the long-established dominance of secular-nationalist political forces would threaten the interests of Indonesia's non-Muslim communities and, ultimately, undermine national cohesion.

While Indonesia's territorial disintegration is not an immediate prospect, neighbouring states and other interested governments have been unable to ignore recent developments in the country. Although there has been no return to the aggressive posture of the Sukarno era, Indonesia's foreign policy has become considerably less coherent and equable since 1998. Post-New Order governments' domestic preoccupations have damaged not just relations with the West and with individual members of the Association of South-east Asian Nations (ASEAN); at a critical phase in its development, ASEAN itself has suffered from Indonesia's inability to maintain its former role as a regional 'first amongst equals'. At the same time, Jakarta's more positive attitude towards Beijing has contributed to China's growing regional influence. Meanwhile, regional governments, particularly Singapore, Malaysia and Australia, together with more geographically distant powers such as Japan, have been concerned over more precise security threats, including secessionism, Islamic terrorism, the movement through Indonesia of asylum-seekers, piracy and environmental threats. However, there are few circumstances in which regional or other powers would see military intervention as both useful and feasible, short of the still-unlikely scenario of Indonesia's disintegration.

Indonesia's multi-dimensional crisis will not be resolved during Megawati's first (and possibly only) part-term as president, and it appears unlikely that a more effective government will emerge as a result of the parliamentary and presidential elections in 2004. Except in the long term, there is little prospect of profound change in the pattern of civil–military relations, or of far-reaching security-sector reform, both of which are needed to resolve Indonesia's separatist and communal conflicts. Severe economic hardship will continue to afflict most Indonesians, pushing more of them towards religious fundamentalism and political extremism. The best that can be hoped for is that the government contains communal and political tensions, while incrementally advancing economic, political and security-sector reforms. The priority for other interested governments should be to support all aspects of the fragile reform process, but particularly security-sector reform, in the hope of eventually helping to create the necessary conditions for the peaceful resolution of the country's many problems.

Chapter 1

Indonesia's multi-dimensional crisis

By the early 1990s, political change in Indonesia was widely anticipated. Steady economic growth, the prospect of economic liberalisation, the growth of indigenous Indonesians' share in the economy, and the gradual evolution of non-governmental organisations and independent political groups seemed likely within the next decade to undermine the dominance of Suharto's New Order state and the military's still-central political role. More immediately, it was clear that Suharto's health was failing and that he was unlikely to remain president beyond the medium term. Nevertheless, the nature and speed of political developments in the late 1990s surprised many observers, as economic collapse compounded existing tensions to produce a momentous political impact.

Suharto's ousting and its consequences

Despite the New Order's economic and social achievements, the gap between Indonesia's rich and poor grew dramatically during the 1990s, and by the middle of the decade political and social tensions were already prompting violence. In mid-1996, the government engineered the removal of Sukarno's daughter, Megawati Sukarnoputri, as leader of the opposition Indonesian Democratic Party (PDI-P), and troops attacked the party's headquarters in Jakarta. At the end of 1996 and again just before the May 1997 general elections, rioting broke out in various parts of the country.

The regime's Golkar organisation won the tightly-controlled elections, as usual with a huge majority. In March 1998, the People's

Consultative Assembly (MPR) automatically approved Suharto's seventh term as president, and appointed B. J. Habibie as vice-president. Habibie had served as technology minister since 1978, and had played a leading role in the government-backed Association of Indonesian Muslim Intellectuals (ICMI) during the 1990s.

It was the regional economic crisis, sparked by the collapse of the Thai baht in July 1997, that galvanised political change. By the end of September, the Indonesian rupiah's value against the US dollar had fallen by almost 40%, and Suharto's government called for aid from the International Monetary Fund (IMF). By January 1998, the rupiah had depreciated by 80%. Inflation and unemployment soared. The economy contracted by more than 13% over the following year. Suharto faced growing pressure to step down, particularly from student demonstrators indignant over the ruling circle's corruption and provoked by a reduction in fuel subsidies. When Suharto visited Cairo for a summit meeting in May 1998, his regime unravelled. Troops shot and killed several student demonstrators in Jakarta, triggering rioting in which more than 1,000 people died. On his return to Jakarta, Suharto found that even his own ministers were turning against him, and he was unable to form a new cabinet. Habibie eventually persuaded him to resign and, with support from General Wiranto, the military commander and defence minister, assumed the presidency as head of an interim administration pending new elections.

Suharto's downfall opened the way for a considerably more open and liberal political system. Habibie initiated significant reforms, including restoring press freedom, releasing political prisoners, introducing legislation allowing for the devolution of political and fiscal authority to the regions, and commencing talks with Portugal over East Timor's future. In June 1999, Indonesia held its first democratic parliamentary elections since 1955. Forty-eight parties contested the elections, compared with the three highly-regulated groupings allowed under the New Order. The polls were largely peaceful, with a 79% turnout and 105 million valid votes cast. At the national level, Megawati's PDI-P won the largest number of votes and seats in the House of Representatives (DPR), but failed to secure a majority. Despite its New Order past, Golkar was the second most successful party, with particularly strong support in eastern Indonesia.

Table 1 Proportion of vote in the June 1999 election and party representation in the House of Representatives

Party	Vote (seats)
PDI-P (Partai Demokrasi Indonesia – Perjuangan) Indonesian Democratic Party – Struggle *Secular nationalist, with particularly strong support in Java and Bali*	35% (153 seats)
Golkar (Golongan Karya) Functional Group party *Nationalist and historically secular, but possessing Islamic credentials; substantial support outside Java*	20% (120 seats)
PKB (Partai Kebangkitan Bangsa) National Awakening Party *Closely linked to Abdurrahman Wahid's traditionalist Islamic mass movement, Nahdlatul Ulama; main support in east and central Java*	17% (51 seats)
PPP (Partai Persatuan Pembangunan) United Development Party *Muslim party allowed under New Order, now projecting orthodox Islamic views and drawing much support from the Muhammadiyah mass movement*	10% (58 seats)
PAN (Partai Amanat Nasional) National Mandate Party *Modernist Islamic party, linked to Muhammadiyah and supported particularly by the urban middle-class*	7% (34 seats)
PBB (Partai Bulan Bintang) Crescent and Star Party *Minor Islamic party favouring imposition of Islamic law*	2% (13 seats)
PK (Partai Keadilan) Justice Party *Minor but radical Islamic party with strong support in Muslim universities in Java*	1% (7 seats)
Other parties	8% (26 seats)
Total elected seats	462
Non-elected seats held by the armed forces and police faction	38
Total DPR seats	**500**

Source: Komisi Pemilihan Umum (General Election Commission) official count at count-stop, 26 July 1999, in 'Provisional Results of the General Elections of June 7, 1999', Max-Planck-Gesselschaft, available at http://w3.rz-berlin.mpg.de/~wm/NUSA/PEMILU/VoteCount.html

Over the following months, party leaders attempted to build support among delegates to the MPR, which convened in October 1999 with the principal purpose of electing a new president. The MPR included all DPR members, along with 130 delegates from the provincial parliaments, also elected in June 1999, and 65 representatives of selected social groups.

In the event, the MPR election took a surprising turn. The UN-backed military intervention in East Timor in September 1999 humiliated Habibie, and a banking scandal involving close associates further damaged his credibility. In October 1999, the MPR rejected Habibie's accountability speech and he withdrew from the presidential contest. Meanwhile, Megawati's aloofness had deprived her of support for her presidential candidacy from beyond her own party and Abdurrahman's National Awakening Party (PKB). The frail and almost blind Abdurrahman, a liberal Muslim intellectual, had been a significant opposition figure under the New Order. In 1991, he had set up the Forum Demokrasi to counter Suharto's efforts to co-opt Muslim political support. Seen as a living saint by his followers, Abdurrahman commanded the loyalty of the 30–40m-strong Islamic mass movement Nahdlatul Ulama (NU), based in East Java.

To other Muslim parties, Megawati was an objectionable candidate because she was not only a secularist, but also a woman. To prevent her from becoming president, a loose coalition of Muslim parties known as the Central Axis, led by the National Mandate Party (PAN)'s Amien Rais, voted for Abdurrahman, who won the MPR election with 373 votes to Megawati's 313. Abdurrahman subsequently supported Megawati's successful vice-presidential candidacy.[1]

Abdurrahman's unstable government

Abdurrahman and Megawati immediately faced major challenges bequeathed by the Suharto and Habibie administrations. The new government's priority was to revive Indonesia's devastated economy, particularly through far-reaching reforms in the banking and corporate sectors. At the same time, it intended to tackle corruption, which was widely believed to have contributed to the economic crisis, and which impeded effective economic restructuring.

Not all of the administration's problems were inherited from its predecessors. Instability within the cabinet underlined the weakness of Abdurrahman's position as a president with little reliable parliamentary support. Nevertheless, the lack of credible presidential and vice-presidential alternatives helped him to retain power during 2000. Despite her party's significant electoral support, non-PDI-P politicians saw Megawati as lacking leadership potential and political vision, and some Muslim political leaders were still reluctant to allow a woman – particularly one regarded as only a nominal Muslim – to become president. Golkar's leader, Akbar Tandjung, was unpopular largely because of his party's New Order associations. The evident political opportunism of Amien Rais, combined with his links to extremist Muslim organisations, undermined his credibility as a potential national leader. Meanwhile, the weakness of Abdurrahman's presidency allowed serious economic, social and political problems to fester. Prominent among these was the armed forces' continuing role in non-military spheres.[2]

Demilitarising politics and depoliticising the military

The New Order's collapse changed the established non-military roles of the armed forces. The inept and brutal actions of elements of the military during the transition to democracy lost the armed forces much popular respect and political legitimacy, while widely-publicised evidence of past abuses further eroded the military's image as the 'soul of the nation'.

Superficial reform under Habibie

After Habibie's installation as president, Wiranto initially acquiesced in political reforms affecting the armed forces. Most importantly, the military's DPR representation was reduced from 75 to 38 seats, and political 'equidistance' replaced the military's close relationship with Golkar. The large number of active and retired military officers assigned to powerful and lucrative bureaucratic and legislative posts was reduced. There were also significant structural changes. In April 1999, the national police force, Polri, was separated from the armed forces, which reverted to their pre-1962 title of Indonesian National Forces (TNI). At the same time, the police were assigned responsibility for internal security. In July 2000, Polri came under the direct control of the president, rather than the defence minister.

Despite these reforms under Habibie, the military retained substantial autonomy and influence. Five cabinet ministers were senior serving officers. Although senior officers talked about developing a 'new paradigm' for the TNI, they exploited the poor security situation to justify a continuing internal-security function and territorial role. The TNI's territorial structure, which paralleled civilian government down to village level, allowed the armed forces to maintain influence in the provinces. This was vital for financial reasons: local business activities provided much of the 75% of TNI funding that came from extra-budgetary sources.[3] Also, TNI businesses substantially supplemented senior officers' official salaries.

Although some senior officers close to the former regime were either dismissed or effectively sidelined, there was no thoroughgoing effort to root out military personnel responsible for human-rights abuses. Nor was there any sign that the TNI intended to abandon its heavy-handed 'security approach', which routinely involved extreme brutality to terrorise people in East Timor, Aceh and Irian Jaya. Events in East Timor in August–September 1999 showed that Habibie's government had no effective control over TNI operations around Indonesia's periphery.

Change and tension Under Abdurrahman

When Abdurrahman became president, it was clear that the TNI's interference in non-military spheres might seriously obstruct the new government's programme.[4] Abdurrahman's initial cabinet included six ministers with TNI backgrounds, of whom four were serving officers. The defence minister was civilian, and the new TNI commander-in-chief, an admiral, was only the second non-army officer ever to hold the post.

These innovations did not, however, fundamentally reduce the military's political influence. Within weeks, tensions between Abdurrahman and the armed forces provoked fears that the TNI might attempt to reassert its power, either directly through a coup or indirectly by creating instability so as to undermine the government's authority. The two immediate points of contention concerned policy in Aceh, where the military favoured a hardline approach despite Abdurrahman's wish for a political settlement, and the proposed prosecution of senior officers for human-rights abuses. In January 2000, after national and UN investigations had highlighted Wiranto's culpability, Abdurrahman announced the general's imminent removal from the cabinet. Wiranto made clear his unwillingness to step down.[5] However, military commanders knew that a coup would jeopardise the Western support essential for economic recovery, and might spark widespread demonstrations in Jakarta and other major cities.[6] After other senior officers backed the president, Wiranto resigned in mid-February 2000.[7] That same month, Abdurrahman intervened in a reshuffle of command and staff appointments to favour reformist officers.[8] Further changes announced in early 2000 included the TNI's relinquishing of its remaining DPR seats by 2004, a reduction in the number of senior military officers, and the introduction of merit as the sole basis for promotion, in place of patronage and political interference. The government also announced that TNI commercial operations would soon be audited.[9]

However, Abdurrahman calculated that to retain the TNI's cooperation, the speed and extent of military reform had to be moderated. His role in the February reshuffle provoked considerable resentment within the officer corps, and the TNI was subsequently allowed considerable leeway in organising its own affairs. In April 2000, the defence minister emphasised that he saw no significant role for civilians within his ministry.[10] He also revealed that the military's business activities could continue as long as they were legal and publicly accountable.[11] The government's authority over regional military commanders also remained tenuous. Although radical reformers within the military argued for the territorial structure's rapid dismantling, more cautious officers favouring a less traumatic, gradual withdrawal from the socio-political sphere predominated. These officers supported the notion of *peran TNI* ('TNI role'), effectively a diluted *dwi fungsi*.[12] In April 2000, Army Chief of Staff General Tyasno Sudarto announced that the army would soon begin withdrawing personnel deployed in a socio-political role from large Javanese cities, though not from the countryside or outer regions.[13] The defence minister envisaged the TNI's withdrawal from socio-political roles taking as long as a decade.[14] Although trials of junior TNI personnel proceeded, it also seemed increasingly likely that senior officers would escape prosecution for human-rights abuses. The president proposed that the armed forces should apologise for their past crimes as part of a reconciliation process aimed at restoring national unity.

Abdurrahman's downfall

Abdurrahman became increasingly beleaguered as he faced criticism for his erratic political style, reputed cronyism, failure to repair the economy and inability to control escalating communal violence and separatism. His fundamental problem as president was his failure to work within the constraints imposed by his limited parliamentary support. Rather than seek the consensus necessary to advance policy, Abdurrahman effectively abandoned coalition government, alienating politicians outside his own party. Ultimately, he attempted to rule in the quasi-monarchical style of Indonesia's first two presidents.[15]

In August 2000, after being censured by the MPR and threatened with impeachment, Abdurrahman apologised for his shortcomings and assigned 'day-to-day management' of the government to Megawati. However, he quickly appointed a new cabinet composed almost entirely of members of his own party and other supporters, aggravating parliamentary opposition. In February 2001, 86% of DPR members voted to censure Abdurrahman, who had by then lost support from both Megawati's PDI-P and the military's parliamentary faction. Supposedly at issue was his implication in two financial scandals, but the real triggers were alarm at the president's inept handling of deteriorating internal security and continuing economic difficulties, combined with his opponents' wish to punish his reluctance to accommodate their interests.

Abdurrahman did everything in his power to defend his presidency. He questioned the legislature's authority, and threatened to launch corruption indictments against his opponents.[16] He also tried to use the army to impose a state of emergency, and warned that at least six provinces might secede and that his supporters might react violently if he was deposed. Banser, the militia attached to the NU's youth wing, ran riot, attacking offices of political parties opposed to the president.[17] Responding to the censure motion, Abdurrahman again apologised, but dismissed the corruption allegations made against him. In April, another censure motion received overwhelming parliamentary support. In May, the president again attempted to impose a national emergency and dissolve the DPR. However, it was evident by then that most senior TNI officers wanted Megawati to take over as president, and the DPR voted overwhelmingly to begin impeachment proceedings on 1 August.

Abdurrahman's final efforts to hold on to power included three cabinet reshuffles between early June and early July. In June, the appointment of a new attorney-general seemed to foreshadow corruption probes against the president's political adversaries. Abdurrahman also replaced the coordinating minister for political, social and security affairs, and attempted unsuccessfully to dismiss the national police commander, both of whom had refused to support an emergency decree.[18] In early July, Abdurrahman again threatened to declare a state of emergency, dissolve parliament and call new elections. On 23 July, he finally acted out these threats, as well as demanding the dissolution of Golkar, a key component of the impeachment movement.[19] The MPR quickly convened in emergency session, and voted overwhelmingly to install Megawati as president. Abdurrahman conceded defeat.

By the end of Abdurrahman's presidency, none of the problems plaguing Indonesia had been resolved. Between 1997 and 2001, the country's international economic standing declined from lower middle-income status to the level of least developed country.[20] Although economic growth had recovered to 4.8% during 2000, by most other measures the economy remained in poor shape. By mid-2001, annual inflation was running at 12% and the national currency had lost almost 20% of its value since the start of the year. Corruption remained endemic.[21] More than 50% of the state budget for 2001 – much more than combined spending on education, health and social security – was allocated to servicing Indonesia's $140 billion foreign debt, threatening Jakarta's ability to meet the budget-deficit target insisted on by the IMF as a condition for the disbursement of $400m in loans. The IMF delayed release of this tranche in December 2000 and again in July 2001 because of the government's failure to meet its economic-reform commitments. Three and a half years after its establishment, the Indonesian Bank Restructuring Agency (IBRA) had done little to raise funds by selling state assets to help reduce the budget deficit, which had ballooned to $8bn by July 2001. Legislators with vested interests had undermined IBRA's capacity to operate effectively by pressing it to sell assets back to local conglomerates which had surrendered them in 1998 to repay debts to the government.[22] Indonesia's political instability and continuing economic crisis under Abdurrahman meant that local and foreign investors' confidence remained low, and the exodus of capital continued.[23] Poor economic conditions further undermined stability. For example, in June 2001 the growing budget deficit necessitated subsidy cuts, forcing fuel prices up by 30% and sparking protests and strikes across Indonesia.[24]

Abdurrahman had also failed to assert civilian control over the armed forces. His weakening political position meant that he and his government had little effective sanction over the TNI's behaviour, let alone scope for enforcing further reforms. As parliamentary opposition to his presidency grew, Abdurrahman highlighted the TNI's continuing political significance by attempting to use it as an instrument to protect his own position. There was no significant progress towards enforcing justice on military perpetrators of past abuses, or ending the TNI's territorial role or commercial activities. The armed forces were no longer as strong or united as they had been under the New Order, but TNI leaders had nevertheless protected their institutional and personal interests. Although senior officers seen as moderate reformers became prominent in the TNI command structure, the military remained sufficiently influential to play a pivotal – if ultimately essentially passive – role in Abdurrahman's ousting.

A third key area of failure was Abdurrahman's inability to control growing separatism and communal conflict. By mid-2001, secessionist impulses were stronger than ever in Aceh and Irian Jaya. TNI policies in these two provinces had done nothing to ameliorate the rebellions, often apparently contradicting Abdurrahman's preference for political solutions. In addition, violence between ethnic and religious groups raged in parts of eastern Indonesia.

Megawati Sukarnoputri: a new beginning ...

Megawati's mandate was considerably stronger than Abdurrahman's. Her share of the vote in 1999 confirmed her as Indonesia's most popular politician, and many of her PDI-P followers believed that, as Sukarno's daughter, she was virtually predestined to lead the country. However, as vice-president she had displayed little political skill and articulated few substantial or original political ideas. She lacked a parliamentary majority, and from the beginning her government was vulnerable to pressure from the political and military interests that had brought her to power.

The strength of alternative political views was clear within days, with the MPR's selection of United Development Party (PPP) Chairman Hamzah Haz as vice-president. Hamzah represented the

Central Axis of Muslim parties that had installed Abdurrahman and prevented Megawati from becoming president in 1999, and had then unseated Abdurrahman. He had campaigned for the amendment of the constitution to include the Jakarta Charter, which would apply *sharia* law to all Muslim Indonesians, and his relations with the avowedly secular Megawati were uneasy. Nevertheless, in early August party leaders, the media and financial markets responded positively when Megawati announced her cabinet, a judicious combination of party representatives (from the Central Axis, Golkar and even Abdurrahman's PKB, as well as the PDI-P) and technocrats, who held all the key economic and financial portfolios.[25]

Megawati also accommodated military interests. Although the defence minister was again a civilian, the TNI was represented in the cabinet by four retired generals. The nationalist outlook of the new president was shared by senior officers, and seemed likely to ensure that Megawati's relations with the TNI would be considerably closer than Abdurrahman's had been. Observers noted Megawati's links with hardline TNI figures such as retired Major-General Theo Syafei, a deputy chairman of the PDI-P.[26] It was widely expected that Megawati's government would be less willing to implement significant reforms affecting the TNI or to prosecute military personnel for past abuses, and more likely to allow the military to crush secessionist movements. Military historian Salim Said even feared that the TNI would now fill 'the vacuum created by weak civilian leadership and prolonged factional infighting'.[27]

Nevertheless, Megawati's 'steady and commanding approach' and surprisingly liberal early initiatives impressed many observers.[28] She outlined a six-point programme for her cabinet, highlighting her principal objectives of:

- maintaining national unity;
- continuing reform and democratisation;
- normalising economic life;
- upholding the law, restoring security and peace, and eradicating corruption and cronyism;
- restoring Indonesia's international credibility; and
- preparing for general elections in 2004.[29]

Megawati's initial public statements seemed to reinforce her reformist credentials. Her emphasis on upholding the rule of law led her to order PDI-P members to declare their assets to an anti-corruption body, and to warn her own family members, as well as ministers and senior state officials, against graft.[30]

In her August 2001 state-of-the-nation address, Megawati proposed convening a commission to 'modernise' the 1945 constitution. After the chaos brought about by Abdurrahman's protracted squabble with parliament, Megawati's initiative opened up the possibility of a clearer separation and demarcation between the powers of the legislative, executive and judicial branches of government. The November 2001 MPR session agreed in principle that, from 2004, the president should be directly elected.[31]

Reform of the armed forces remained a live political issue, with many PDI-P members and other Megawati supporters remaining fundamentally anti-military. Standing up to the military on some issues also allowed Megawati to demonstrate her reformist credentials to the US and other Western governments. Although Megawati stressed the importance of Indonesia's territorial cohesion, she apologised for military abuses in Aceh and Irian Jaya, and called for the TNI to pay greater attention to human rights.[32] The new government expanded judicial investigations into atrocities in East Timor, and declared that military personnel guilty of 'gross violations' would stand trial.[33] In addition, Megawati ordered the TNI to reassess its dual-function doctrine, and emphasised that it must eventually withdraw entirely from politics.

Megawati also stressed the need to restore a reliable banking system and to respect commitments to international creditors. The IMF was impressed with the new government's focus on 'core areas necessary to sustain ... economic recovery', and in August 2001 authorised the $400m loan withheld since December 2000.[34] In early September, the outline of the 2002 budget allocated almost 40% of spending to debt repayment and slashed subsidies. International confidence in Indonesia grew. In late 2001, the Paris Club of creditors rescheduled $2.8bn-worth of debt, and the Consultative Group on Indonesia (an umbrella group of aid donors) promised more than $3bn of fresh loans for development projects.[35]

... Or another step towards chaos?

Despite these moves, a dramatic recovery in Indonesia's fortunes was unlikely under Megawati's government. Senior cabinet ministers appeared indecisive and lacked urgency in their pursuit of the economic, political and security objectives set by Megawati. Critics pointed to Megawati's own lack of effective, assertive leadership, particularly her over-delegation and lack of day-to-day involvement in policy-making.[36] The global economic downturn combined with the economic and security implications of the 11 September attacks in the US made the new government's tasks even more difficult.[37]

Indonesia's economic prospects did not seem to improve significantly during 2001. Despite initially increased international confidence, perceptions of high political risk, rampant corruption and an inadequate legal framework continued to deter foreign investment, which fell by 43%.[38] Economic growth reached just 3.3%, and unemployment, already at 40m, continued to grow. At the same time, the 50% of the population living in poverty suffered as inflation increased to 14%.[39] By late 2001, concern was also mounting over the government's failure to generate sufficient proceeds from asset sales and privatisation, partly because DPR legislators and state-sector employees often objected to foreign investment.[40] Provincial politicians were also obstructive; for instance, West Sumatran legislators took control of the local branch of the national cement industry rather than allow its sale to a multinational company.[41]

Despite the accommodation of new political forces and the TNI's reduced political role, many Indonesians still see Megawati's administration as protecting the interests of the Suharto-era ruling élite. As one former cabinet minister put it, 'It's the New Order without the leadership and without the vision'.[42] In particular, the failure to bring corrupt officials and bankers to justice undermined local and international confidence in the new government's will and ability to uphold the law.[43] Within days of Megawati becoming president, the judge who had sentenced Suharto's son Hutomo ('Tommy') Mandala Putra to jail for corruption was murdered, apparently by contract killers. In October 2001, the Supreme Court overturned the original ruling against Tommy, who since November 2000 had eluded police efforts to arrest him. He was finally arrested in November 2001, and in March 2002 stood trial for conspiracy to murder and illegal possession of weapons. However, by April 2002 the defection of key witnesses had again cast doubt on whether justice would prevail.[44] In another high-profile case, Akbar Tandjung, Golkar chairman and DPR speaker, was finally detained in March

2002 over long-standing allegations of corruption. However, Akbar retained his DPR post even while in custody, and was released on bail after a month. It was widely suspected in Jakarta that the minor flurry of arrests and trials in early 2002 was aimed mainly at impressing a meeting of Paris Club creditors scheduled for April.[45]

There were also limits to how far Megawati and her government were willing and able to assert control over the military. In August 2001, Megawati authorised the trial of military and police officers in cases including crimes in East Timor in 1999. However, the first five officers were not charged until March 2002, amid speculation that the government had delayed the trial to win military support and that political considerations had influenced the selection of judges.[46] Meanwhile, TNI personnel and TNI-sponsored militias continued to commit serious abuses while executing heavy-handed internal-security operations, particularly in Aceh. Megawati's efforts in late 2001 and early 2002 to replace the TNI commander, Admiral Widodo Adisucipto, with a more amenable officer underlined the TNI's continuing political importance.[47] By this time, it was clear that Megawati and many senior TNI officers shared a common interest in containing a perceived growing threat from Islamic extremists in the run-up to the 2004 elections.

The future of Megawati's government

Despite widespread disappointment within and outside Indonesia over her government's early performance, Megawati is likely to survive as president until the presidential election in 2004. By November 2001, she was stressing economic recovery, political 'normalization' and law enforcement ahead of further reform and democratisation.[48] She will probably continue to avoid confrontation with parliament and the state apparatus, including the TNI, by not pressing too hard for reform. Even though a dispute with Vice-President Hamzah erupted in May 2002 over his close links with Islamic militants, Megawati seemed determined to prioritise governmental consensus and national stability.

Economic difficulties may, however, provoke further political instability. Indonesia's daunting array of domestic problems will continue to deter the foreign investment so vital for economic recovery. While 6–7% growth is needed just to create sufficient employment for new entrants to the labour market, only 3–3.5%

expansion was expected in 2002. Meanwhile, government spending cuts will be necessary to control the budget deficit. Subsidies, which accounted for almost one-fifth of government spending in 2001, were to be reduced substantially during 2002. Public reaction to three increases in petrol prices, caused by successive subsidy cuts in early 2002, was muted. Anticipated reductions in food and kerosene subsidies could, however, provoke major demonstrations.[49]

While economic hardship may undermine popular support for Megawati and her administration, it is unlikely that her political rivals will attempt to exploit this to oust her before 2004. Indonesia's other leading politicians are preoccupied above all with accumulating funds and support in advance of the 2004 elections. However, by late 2001 the emergence of intra-party feuds had complicated the picture. The problems of Golkar, the second-largest parliamentary party, were particularly acute: with its chairman Akbar Tandjung discredited and other leaders facing corruption investigations, the party seemed to be on the brink of disintegrating into factions representing the interests of the eastern provinces, reformers, bureaucrats and retired TNI officers.[50] The build-up to the 2004 DPR elections may see new alliances between various parties' factions, and even the emergence of new parties. Meanwhile, despite the TNI's overall conservatism, autonomy and continuing political influence, its fear of negative domestic and international reaction as well as Islamic extremism suggest that military support for any challenge to Megawati's leadership is unlikely.

Indonesia is not a 'failed state', but Indonesian politics will continue to suffer from weakness and ineffectiveness at the political centre. Megawati's government will almost certainly be allowed to muddle on, but what many Indonesians call the country's 'multi-dimensional' (economic, social, political and security) crisis will continue until 2004, and almost certainly beyond. One of the most important likely consequences is that secessionism and communal violence will continue in the country's periphery. At the same time, long-term economic hardship, exacerbated by tough fiscal policies and the lack of effective grass-roots development strategies, may intensify social breakdown and political conflict in Indonesia's Javanese centre, particularly between secular and Muslim political forces.

Chapter 2

Managing separatism

Since Suharto's ousting, and particularly since the UN-backed military intervention in East Timor in September 1999, international reportage and analysis have highlighted the growth of strong centrifugal forces within Indonesia, often claiming that the country might fragment along the lines of the Soviet Union and Yugoslavia.[1] Senior military officers and political leaders in Indonesia have also emphasised this danger. General Tyasno Sudarto warned in January 2000 that the 'threat of national disintegration' required 'immediate attention'.[2] Amien Rais claimed in October 2000 that 'the threat of disintegration' obsessed him.[3] Soon afterwards, the National Resilience Institute's governor, Lieutenant-General Johny Lumintang, spoke of 'the nation's disintegration coming close to reality'.[4] While he was president, Abdurrahman expended considerable energy on securing other governments' support for Indonesia's territorial integrity. Subsequently, Megawati has made maintaining national unity her government's primary objective. However, East Timor was an exceptional case and its separation did not necessarily provide a precedent for other provinces. Although special autonomy arrangements for Aceh and Papua (known until recently as Irian Jaya), where secessionists have long pursued armed struggles, is unlikely to blunt separatist demands, there is little likelihood that local rebels can defeat the TNI. Elsewhere in Indonesia, administrative and fiscal decentralisation promises to help undermine separatist sentiment, but it may also stimulate new problems.

Map 2 Indonesia's provinces

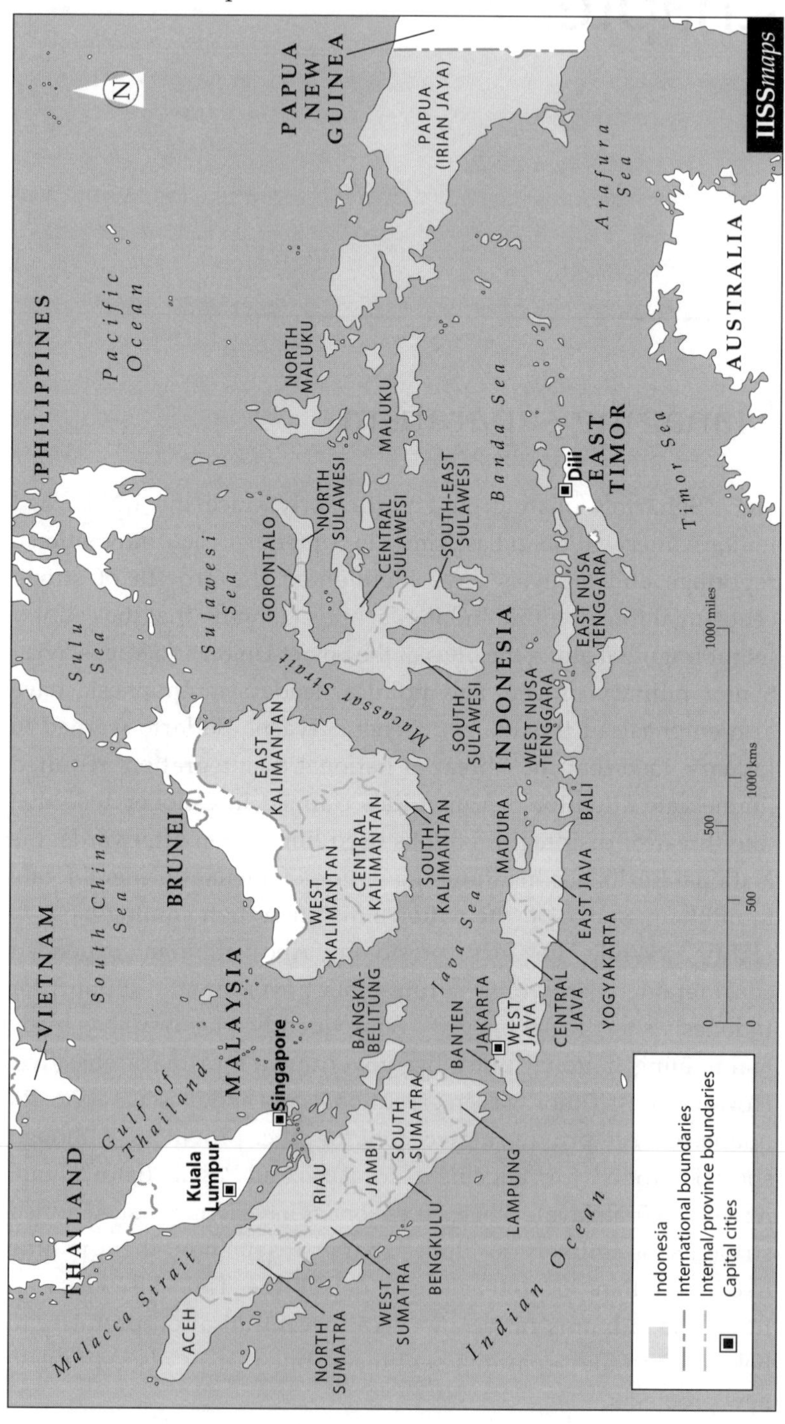

Challenges to the unitary state

While the issue has become particularly acute since 1998, problems of national cohesion predated Suharto's fall. Indonesia's size, cultural diversity and lack of direct pre-colonial antecedents have long forced its leaders to work hard to foster a sense of national identity. The question of whether Indonesia should be a unitary or a federal state was central to nationalist debates during the late colonial period. In 1949, the Dutch transferred sovereignty to the federal Republic of the United States of Indonesia (RUSI). The federation included all areas of the Netherlands East Indies except West New Guinea (later Irian Jaya, now called Papua), which remained under Dutch control. RUSI survived for just eight months. After an attempted coup against the nationalists' Indonesian Republic, which controlled large areas of Java and Sumatra, Sukarno proclaimed a new, unitary Republic of Indonesia in August 1950. Some of the states left behind by the Dutch surrendered their powers without a struggle, while others, notably Eastern Indonesia, resisted what they saw as the imposition of Javanese rule, and armed rebellions broke out in South Sulawesi and on Ambon. Although the rebellion on Ambon had been crushed by November 1950, guerrilla warfare continued on nearby Seram until 1963.[5] Among radical Muslims in West Java, dissatisfaction was evident from 1948, when the Darul Islam (House of Islam) movement was established, with the objective of a federal Islamic state. By 1954, Darul Islam's influence extended into Central Java, South Sulawesi and Aceh, and it controlled much of rural West Java until 1962, when its leader was captured.

A more serious threat to the unitary state emerged after Prime Minister Ali Sastroamidjojo's government took power in 1956. The new administration's economic policies disadvantaged outer islands' export producers, and its composition marginalised the country's largest Muslim political party, Masjumi, which was particularly strong outside Java. Masjumi supporters and local military commanders also resented Sukarno's increasingly assertive left-wing radicalism. In 1956, commanders in Sumatra and Eastern Indonesia cut links with Jakarta and proclaimed martial law.[6] The aim of these rebellions, which were encouraged and materially supported by the US, Britain and the newly-independent Malayan Federation, was not secession, but rather to redistribute political power and economic benefits from the centre to the outer islands. By mid-1958, however, these revolts had been brought under control.

Sukarno used the rebellions in Sumatra and Eastern Indonesia as the justification for proclaiming nationwide martial law and effectively ending parliamentary democracy.[7] These measures laid the foundations for reintroducing a strongly presidential constitution and imposing the authoritarian Guided Democracy system in 1959. But while Guided Democracy substantially curtailed regional parliaments' powers, during the 1960s 'the dissident regions found that they could make common cause with the anti-Communist military ... in their continuing struggles with the centre'.[8] Consequently, a form of unacknowledged and informal fiscal federalism evolved, involving compromises between local officials, the military and central-government civil servants, under which proceeds from illegal taxes and smuggling were shared.[9]

Under Suharto's New Order regime, particularly from the early 1970s, the central government's growing financial strength allowed much greater centralisation of economic power. The Regional Government Law of 1974 further tightened the centre's political control. At the same time, the regime successfully operated a system of regional grants and subsidies to local administrations which allowed significant infrastructural development in many provinces.[10] Combined with the state's repressive political controls and extensive security apparatus, these programmes contained centrifugal forces. By the late 1980s, however, criticism of the New Order's regional funding system was growing, particularly from resource-rich provinces, which retained little of the wealth that they generated.[11] During the 1980s, for instance, more than half of Irian Jaya's regional product was exported to other provinces or abroad, and more than 60% of gross domestic product (GDP) drained out of resource-rich Aceh. The economist Anne Booth notes that 'if a higher proportion of the revenues from gas exploitation were allowed to stay in the province, living standards in Aceh would be much closer to those of Malaysia'.[12] Similarly, there was considerably more poverty in East Kalimantan than in the neighbouring Malaysian state of Sabah.

During the early 1990s, concern in Jakarta that over-centralisation might undermine national cohesion prompted a series of decentralisation initiatives. These measures were, however, superficial: while they devolved responsibility for implementing local-government functions to 'second level' regional administrations (regencies and cities), decision-making powers remained in Jakarta.[13] By this time, military force was already a prominent instrument for maintaining control in the face of armed rebellions in East Timor, Aceh and Irian Jaya.

East Timor: a precedent?

In 1999, Indonesia was forced to concede defeat in East Timor. In January, Habibie surprised Indonesians, East Timorese and the world by announcing that the inhabitants of East Timor would be allowed to vote in a plebiscite on an Indonesian government proposal which would yield substantial autonomy to the territory. If the East Timorese rejected the proposal, Habibie would recommend to the MPR that the territory be allowed to secede. In the August 1999 referendum, 78.5% voted against autonomy, and thus effectively in favour of independence.

Widespread violence both before and during the referendum, sponsored by the military and carried out by local pro-Indonesian militias, left more than 1,000 civilians dead and much of East Timor's infrastructure destroyed. In response, Australian and other foreign forces intervened in September 1999, effectively liberating the territory. This deeply humiliated Habibie's government and the TNI, and ensured that Indonesia had no choice but to relinquish control of the territory. Following a period of UN administration, democratic elections to a Constituent Assembly were held in August 2001, and East Timor became independent in May 2002. Fretilin, the nationalist movement which had long resisted Indonesia's occupation, secured 55 of the 88 Assembly seats, and will dominate East Timor's post-independence government.[14]

Although events in East Timor may well have encouraged separatists in Aceh and Irian Jaya, parallels with other restless provinces are not convincing: East Timor was an exceptional case in several ways. Indonesia's founding fathers had never seriously envisaged this Portuguese colony becoming part of their country. Although some of its people have favoured integration, East Timor's different colonial history meant that the great majority did not identify with Indonesia, and consistently supported independence. The scale, intensity and unity of opposition were considerably greater than in Aceh or Irian Jaya. Moreover, there was originally no compelling economic rationale for East Timor's subjugation.

Although the TNI developed significant commercial interests there and the future exploitation of oil resources in the Timor Gap promised substantial returns, the territory was never seen as important for Indonesia's economic survival.

The East Timor question's international dimension was also exceptional. Although a minority of UN members, including Australia and New Zealand, recognised East Timor's inclusion in Indonesia, the majority never formally endorsed its annexation. Indeed, there was widespread international support for East Timor's right to self-determination. For many years, this support came principally from non-governmental lobby groups in the West. However, after the Dili massacre in 1991, when Indonesian troops killed several hundred unarmed East Timorese, public opinion forced Western governments to take greater interest. The August 1999 referendum took place under UN supervision, and the Australian-led military intervention the following month was approved by the UN Security Council and received widespread international support.

East Timor's separation was undoubtedly a blow to Indonesian national pride. But the original primary reason for Indonesia's occupation – fear that the territory might become a vector of communist influence in the immediate aftermath of the collapse of anti-communist forces in Indochina – was no longer relevant after the end of the Cold War. Indeed, by undermining relations with Western governments East Timor had become a burden on Indonesia's foreign policy. In 1999, many Indonesian politicians and senior military officers found it hard to accept the notion of allowing East Timor the option of independence. However, Indonesia's political élite had lost the will to sustain a long-term counter-insurgency campaign in the face of international condemnation. Habibie and the TNI hoped that the offer of autonomy would pacify both the Timorese people and Western governments. While the mayhem of September 1999 highlighted some TNI elements' resistance to East Timor's separation, the armed forces ultimately acquiesced in the Australian-led intervention which paved the way for independence.

Aceh: secession or autonomy?

In Aceh, a pervasive sense of economic injustice combined with a strong tradition of regional self-assertion has produced fierce resistance to Jakarta's control since the late 1980s. Once a powerful Islamic sultanate, Aceh was one of the last parts of the archipelago to fall under Dutch control, in 1913. During the 1920s and 1930s, political activity focused around the All-Aceh Union of Religious Teachers (PUSA). In the aftermath of the Japanese occupation of 1942–45, PUSA overthrew the traditional, pro-Dutch land-owning nobility, and ran Aceh as an autonomous Islamic state during the Indonesian revolution of 1945–49. Acehnese leaders supported the Indonesian nationalist cause, but expected that the new state would recognise their region's distinct history and status.[15] This did not happen, and since 1949 the relationship between Jakarta and Aceh has been tense and often violent.

From 1953, Aceh was an important base for the Darul Islam movement, which subsumed PUSA. The central government's response included making Aceh a province in its own right in 1957, and two years later assigning it 'special region' status, which allowed autonomy in religion, customary law and education. Although many Acehnese welcomed the anti-communist New Order in the mid-1960s, Suharto's centralisation of political and economic power during the 1970s and 1980s provoked resentment. The most important complaint concerned the exploitation of the province's huge natural-gas resources, which benefited the central government at Aceh's expense. During the 1970s, the Lhokseumawe Industrial Zone (ZILS) was created, based on the Arun refinery operated by the US-based multinational Mobil (now ExxonMobil) on behalf of Indonesia's state oil company, Pertamina. The zone created an enclave economy and destroyed traditional livelihoods, while most skilled workers came from other provinces, causing discontent amongst displaced Acehnese villagers. Large-scale pollution and the depletion of forest resources caused serious environmental damage.[16]

In 1976, Hasan di Tiro, a former Darul Islam envoy and businessman descended from pre-colonial sultans, established the Aceh-Sumatra Liberation Front. The organisation soon began operations under the name of the Free Aceh Movement (GAM). Although GAM's early activities were largely limited to propaganda and flag-raising, Jakarta responded by crushing it militarily. By the late 1980s, GAM had re-established itself as an underground political and military force with considerable popular support, and in 1989 it began attacking Indonesian security forces. The rebels, numbering approximately 750, reportedly received significant external support. Libya trained several hundred GAM guerrillas in the late 1980s, and funding came from Acehnese emigrés in Malaysia.[17]

The Indonesian authorities' response to GAM's insurgency was brutal and, in the short term, effective. In mid-1990, 6,000 troops from Army Strategic Command (Kostrad) and the Special Forces Command (Kopassus) were deployed, doubling Indonesia's military strength in Aceh. From then until 1998, the province was designated a Military Operations Area (DOM). Jakarta made no political or economic concessions, and the security forces relied largely on terror: arbitrary detention, beatings, torture, rape and 'disappearances' were widespread. Between 1989 and 1991, the security forces killed approximately 2,000 Acehnese, the great majority of them unarmed civilians.[18] Although sporadic military clashes continued, by late 1991 Indonesia's forces had largely suppressed the rebellion. But the DOM period provoked hostility in most Acehnese, including many who did not support GAM. The regional economic crisis in 1997–98 exacerbated tension in the province, as Acehnese emigrants repatriated from Malaysia strained local resources.[19]

Rapprochement between Jakarta and Aceh seemed possible following the collapse of Suharto's regime. In August 1998, the Indonesian military revoked Aceh's DOM status, and began withdrawing non-territorial forces, including Kopassus. But these measures did not assuage Acehnese resentment. In November 1998, amid provocation by both sides, GAM resumed military operations, and a new Indonesian offensive began in January 1999. Despite the Habibie government's promise to prosecute military personnel for abuses, atrocities continued, notably the murder of an Islamic teacher and 57 of his students in July 1999. By mid-1999, renewed conflict had created more than 100,000 internal refugees.[20] Most Acehnese boycotted the June 1999 elections. Nevertheless, the lifting of the New Order's political repression allowed student and NGO activism to flourish, even in Aceh. The Aceh Referendum Information Centre (SIRA), which called for a referendum on Aceh's future, became an alternative, non-violent focus for independence aspirations. There were also hopes that direct negotiations between Jakarta and GAM could end the violence. In mid-1999, the two sides began talks in Geneva, funded by the US and the UN.[21]

Following his election as president in October 1999, Abdurrahman, who sympathised with Acehnese calls for justice, ordered the TNI to reduce its presence, and established an independent commission intended to bring military human-rights abusers to trial. In early November, SIRA organised a rally attended by around a million Acehnese, a quarter of the population, to demand a referendum.[22] After encountering military opposition, Abdurrahman claimed that any referendum would not concern independence (which was 'out of the question'), but rather the implementation of *sharia* law in the province.[23] Although Acehnese are mainly devout Muslims, most saw this proposal, which was soon quietly abandoned, as evading the central issues of political and economic relations between Aceh and Jakarta. The government subsequently confirmed, however, that new 'special autonomy' legislation would eventually give provincial governments in Aceh and Irian Jaya greater political autonomy and financial resources than other regions would receive under the proposed nationwide devolution of administrative and fiscal powers.[24]

In May 2000, Indonesian and GAM representatives at the Geneva talks agreed a three-month ceasefire, referred to as a 'humanitarian pause', intended to facilitate relief efforts and act as a confidence-building measure. In September, the ceasefire was extended until mid-January 2001.[25] However, in three rounds of talks during 2000 neither side made significant concessions. GAM rejected autonomy and demanded an independence referendum monitored by international observers. Neither Abdurrahman nor the TNI was willing to allow such a plebiscite, as it would almost certainly take Aceh in the same direction as East Timor. For Indonesia's political and military leaders, Aceh was a cornerstone of national unity. According to Amien Rais, Aceh's loss 'would be tantamount to the end of Indonesia as a nation'.[26] The province's economic importance reinforced the determination not to allow a referendum. Although natural-gas reserves were running down, they still contributed the bulk of the $2–3bn-worth of annual revenues from Aceh's natural resources, 95% of which accrued to Jakarta.

The supposed ceasefire did not significantly restrict violence by either side: during 2000, the conflict caused 1,000 deaths, mostly among unarmed civilians, compared with fewer than 400 during 1999.[27] In October–November 2000, the security forces killed 41

Map 3 Aceh

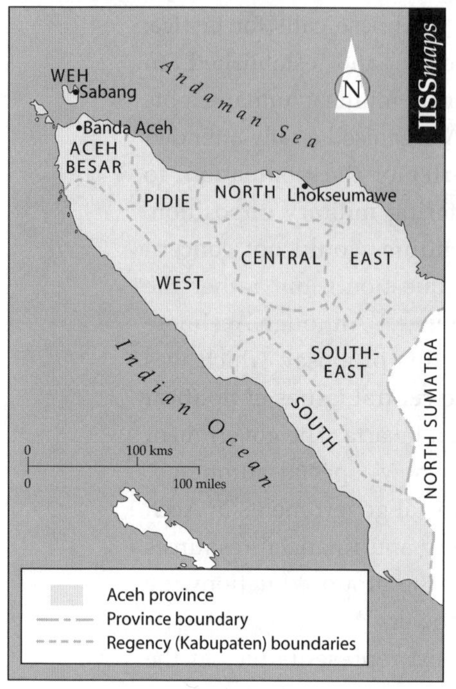

people while trying to prevent Acehnese from attending a second SIRA-organised rally. By the end of 2000, Indonesian security forces in Aceh – numbering roughly 30,000 personnel, including 16,000 TNI troops – were 'engaged in a brutal out-of-control campaign to squash the separatist movement'.[28] Because the police had become responsible for internal security following their separation from the armed forces in 1999, they were formally in charge of security operations in Aceh. However, they lacked adequate training and firepower to operate effectively against GAM, so the regional police commander relied heavily on TNI support.[29] Meanwhile, GAM grew in strength and popular support. By late 2000, it deployed several thousand armed guerrillas (and many more unarmed auxiliaries) and had taken over most civil administration outside the provincial capital, to the extent of routinely collecting taxes. While backing for GAM – itself responsible for widespread intimidation and atrocities, particularly against non-Acehnese – was not universal in Aceh, SIRA claimed that an unofficial poll of more than two million Acehnese in November 2000 showed 92% favouring independence.[30]

Amid the security operations, there was still a political dimension to Jakarta's policies. In November 2000, Abdurrahman's administration announced that it would ask the DPR to draft 'special autonomy' legislation based on a proposal from Aceh's provincial parliament, implying significant political and economic concessions. Further negotiations in Geneva in January–February 2001 replaced the 'humanitarian pause' with 'Peace through Dialogue', involving an indefinite ceasefire extension and agreement that all-inclusive political dialogue was desirable. As a confidence-building measure, TNI and GAM field commanders established telephone 'hotlines'.[31] However, neither side indicated a willingness to compromise on Aceh's sovereignty.

As Abdurrahman's position became increasingly precarious in early 2001, senior TNI officers stepped up demands for a military offensive against GAM. In March 2001, ExxonMobil temporarily halted production at Arun out of concern at the deteriorating security situation. This was a serious blow to dependent industries in the ZILS, and to the confidence of Indonesia's main natural-gas customers in Japan and South Korea.[32] The disruption of this 'strategic facility' also provided additional justification for a greater TNI role in suppressing GAM.[33] Almost immediately, the army deployed more than 2,000 troops to strengthen the plant's security.

In April 2001, Presidential Instruction 4/2001 attempted to reconcile Jakarta's political and security approaches to the Acehnese problem by authorising draconian military measures under the 'political umbrella' of a supposedly comprehensive six-pronged approach to restoring security.[34] An Aceh Security Command was established to centralise control over police and TNI forces, and the military deployed 1,500 troops, drawn mainly from Kostrad. While these fresh forces had supposedly received special training in human rights and were issued with stricter rules of engagement, the increased military presence apparently sharpened the conflict, and large numbers of civilians fell victim to security-force brutality.[35] Confidence-building measures languished as the military campaign escalated from early May. New talks in Geneva in July were inconclusive, and another round scheduled for September 2001 did not take place. Discussions in Aceh in July to establish a bilateral ceasefire-supervision committee failed to make progress. Police then arrested six GAM negotiators.[36]

After Megawati's accession to power in July 2001, she and her government appeared to assign greater priority to solving Aceh's problems. In mid-August, the new president apologised to the people of Aceh for past policies, particularly human-rights abuses. In the same month, Megawati signed into law the long-anticipated special autonomy bill. Four key provisions of the law were that:

- the provincial government's share of oil and gas revenues would increase from 5% to 70%;
- there would be direct elections for the provincial governorship and other local-government posts;

- the governor would possess veto rights over senior military appointments in Aceh; and
- the provincial government would be allowed to introduce elements of *sharia* law.[37]

Although the new law failed to impress most Acehnese, representatives in national and local parliaments together with many better-educated urban Acehnese welcomed the prospect of special autonomy, which took effect in January 2002.[38] However, the gulf between the positions of Jakarta and GAM remained. There was no sign that the special autonomy law, rejected by GAM, had affected the conflict. Indeed, GAM's control of rural areas seemed likely to delay or even prevent the implementation of many of the new law's provisions. GAM continued to attack the security forces, while Kostrad's commander claimed in August 2001 that the military's objective was now GAM's 'total annihilation'.[39] Following complaints from ExxonMobil over continuing threats to the security of its plant, which had resumed operations, Kopassus launched 'search and destroy' missions in October, with the neutralisation of GAM commander Tengku Abdullah Syafi'ie as a primary objective.[40] Ominously, 'militia groups armed, trained and financed by the military', and often comprising non-Acehnese, were becoming more widespread.[41] Unidentified assassins – possibly military-intelligence operatives – murdered public figures including local legislators, a climate of fear pervaded the province and economic and infrastructural disruption was widespread. GAM continued to extort funding from the population and to victimise non-Acehnese residents, many of whom fled the province.

One factor explaining the military crackdown may have been that, as the US widened its 'war against terrorism' to include South-east Asia, there seemed less reason to worry that Washington would object to firm measures against GAM, which was widely if erroneously seen in the West as an Islamic fundamentalist movement. The Megawati government's acquiescence in the military's tougher posture was confirmed in late November 2001, when Coordinating Minister for Political and Security Affairs Susilo Bambang Yudhoyono announced that large numbers of military and police personnel would be deployed to major trouble-spots, including Aceh. Susilo claimed that separatist movements would be 'stopped once and for all':

the government would no longer 'compromise' with GAM.[42] Approximately 1,600 people were killed in Aceh during 2001.[43]

In January 2002, Jakarta announced that a separate military area command would be re-established in Aceh to control larger numbers of permanently-based troops.[44] In late January, Tengku Abdullah Syafi'ie was killed, and GAM appeared to be on the defensive.[45] In February, the rebels accepted special autonomy as a starting-point for negotiations, and agreed to a new ceasefire and confidence-building measures in advance of the 2004 provincial elections.[46] If special autonomy can ameliorate economic injustice and increase popular support for the provincial government, it might ultimately reduce the appeal of independence. However, this could probably only be achieved if Jakarta demonstrated commitment to implementing the new law's provisions comprehensively, involved local communities in development projects and halted security-force abuses and brought their perpetrators to justice.[47] The Indonesian government seems unlikely to meet these conditions in the foreseeable future, and armed conflict seems set to continue.[48]

Papua: the Melanesian rebellion

At the archipelago's other extreme, post-New Order developments in Papua have challenged Jakarta's control almost as seriously as the Acehnese revolt. As in Aceh, Indonesia's favoured instruments – military repression and 'special autonomy' – have done nothing to stem secessionist sentiment.

The Netherlands prevented West New Guinea, as Papua was then known, from joining Indonesia in 1949, largely out of concern for the welfare of the territory's Melanesian people, who were ethnically distinct from Indonesia's population and included many Christians. Most Indonesian nationalists, however, believed that the territory rightfully belonged to their country. During the 1950s, the Dutch allowed elections to a New Guinea Council, and in 1961 local political leaders unilaterally declared the independence of 'West Papua'. However, an Indonesian politico-military campaign against continued Dutch control provoked US diplomatic intervention and, ultimately, agreement that the territory would be transferred to UN authority in October 1962, followed by a hand-over to Indonesian control from May 1963. It was also agreed that, within six years, there should be a UN-supervised 'Act of Free Choice', in which the

Map 4 Papua (Irian Jaya)

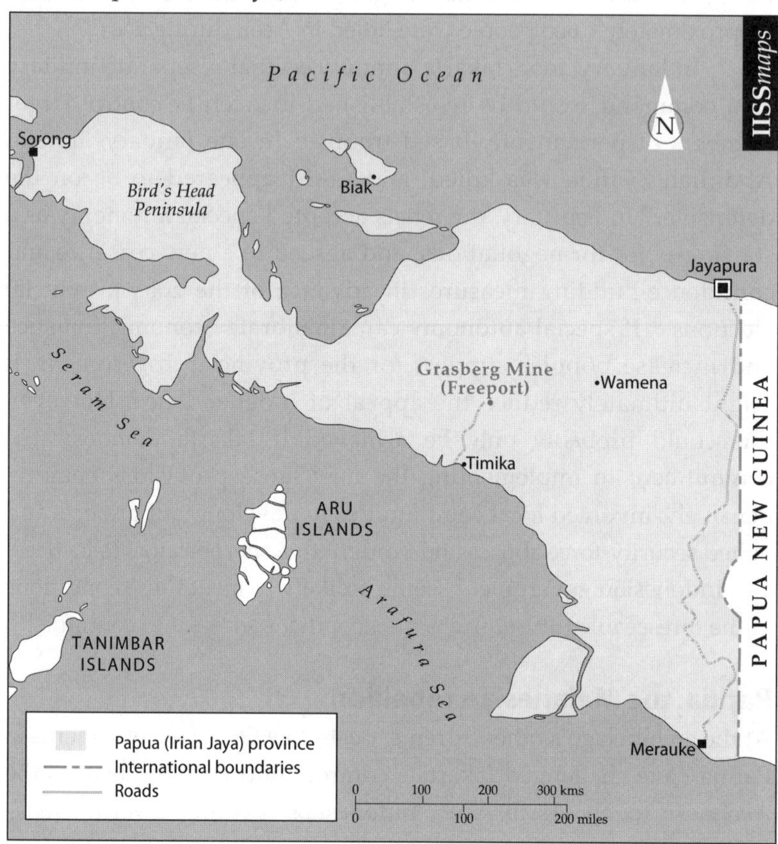

population could accept or reject integration with Indonesia. In the event, Indonesia assumed full control as soon as it could in 1963. When the plebiscite was finally held, in 1969, it was a stage-managed affirmation of Indonesian rule by a selection of intimidated tribal leaders. In November 1969, the UN General Assembly endorsed Indonesia's incorporation of the territory.

In 1962, anti-Indonesian dissidents founded the Papua Youth Movement. By 1964, this had evolved into the Papua Freedom Movement (OPM), which subsequently mounted sporadic armed opposition to what most local people saw as Indonesia's illegitimate occupation. Jakarta's policy of encouraging migration into the territory from densely-populated regions, mainly Java and Sulawesi, exacerbated the indigenous population's secessionism. By the late

1990s, the mainly Muslim migrants constituted around one-third of the province's total population of 2.5m, and dominated local commerce. The exploitation of Irian Jaya's natural resources, particularly the massive US- and British-owned Freeport copper and gold mine, further heightened resentment. At the same time, the Freeport mine, which began operations in 1972 and soon became one of Indonesia's largest sources of revenue, underlined Irian Jaya's importance to Jakarta.

After the neighbouring Australian-administered territory of Papua New Guinea (PNG) achieved independence in 1975, OPM's small guerrilla army received limited support from across the border. However, PNG's government prioritised stable relations with Jakarta ahead of solidarity with OPM. Although OPM proved an irritant to the New Order regime and its armed forces, tribally-based factionalism seriously weakened its leadership. Jakarta's security forces routinely committed abuses while suppressing OPM, its sympathisers and other anti-Indonesian political activists. Human-rights groups claim that Indonesian forces have killed more than 100,000 people in the province since 1963.[49] By the mid-1990s, OPM had been reduced to two tribally-based bands operating close to the PNG border, but resentment against Indonesian control and exploitation remained widespread. Suharto's overthrow and East Timor's separation stimulated the growth of pro-independence movements. The 31-strong Papuan Presidium Council (PDP) brought together leading secessionists. Although the PDP sought to achieve independence peacefully, it was loosely linked to the 22,000-strong Satgas Papua (Task Force Papua), which grouped together pro-independence tribal militias.

As president, Abdurrahman attempted to come to terms with separatism in Irian Jaya. Although he ruled out independence, massive pro-independence demonstrations in the province in November 1999 prompted several conciliatory gestures. Abdurrahman apologised for past abuses, promised 'special autonomy', declared that the province's name should be changed to Papua, recognised the PDP's representative legitimacy, and even provided financial support for a Papuan People's Congress organised by the PDP in May–June 2000. The Congress was attended by 2,700 activists and tribal leaders. Embarrassingly for Abdurrahman, it declared Indonesia's incorporation of Irian Jaya invalid and called for international recognition of Papua's sovereignty.[50]

Jakarta flatly rejected the Congress' declaration, but in another token gesture announced that the Morning Star flag (an important and hitherto illegal symbol of independence) could be flown in the province alongside Indonesia's.[51] This merely exacerbated an already tense situation, and over the following months flag-raising by separatists provoked numerous clashes with Indonesian forces. In October 2000, Satgas Papua members killed at least 28 non-Papuans in the highland town of Wamena after police removed Morning Star flags and killed several militiamen.[52]

The Wamena incident led Jakarta to ban the separatist flag. It was also used to justify tougher security policies, which senior TNI and intelligence officers had devised in June 2000 in response to the People's Congress.[53] Extra troops and police were deployed, bringing total security-force numbers in the province to more than 10,000. At the same time, there was growing evidence that the TNI was nurturing pro-Indonesian militias among non-Papuans.[54] In November 2000, police arrested PDP leaders, including chairman Theys Hiu Eluay, on sedition charges. As Satgas Papua activists clashed more frequently with Indonesian security forces and non-Papuan migrants, the PDP called for UN military and diplomatic intervention to end the violence and mediate a political settlement.[55] During 2001, OPM forces stepped up operations on the PNG frontier, taking hostages and attacking Indonesian troops. For several days in October, 400–500 OPM guerrillas and tribesmen seized control of a district capital.

Meanwhile, Abdurrahman's government had drawn up special-autonomy legislation, intended, as in Aceh, to undermine secessionist aspirations by devolving substantial administrative and fiscal authority. In January 2001, Irian Jaya's provincial government and parliament, together with local NGOs, began drafting their own version of the Special Autonomy Bill, including provisions for local legislators to veto the deployment of Indonesian security forces, the establishment of a local police force, and the thorough investigation of and compensation for human-rights abuses.[56] Many separatists rejected autonomy, and most delegates to a provincial forum in March 2001 demanded a referendum on independence.[57] Others indicated interest in negotiating a settlement if this involved not only special autonomy, but also the province's demilitarisation and Jakarta's acceptance that the independence struggle would continue by peaceful means.[58]

In June 2001, Indonesia's national parliament, which by then was in confrontation with the president, decided to deliberate the locally-drafted autonomy bill alongside the central government's version. The special-autonomy law that parliament approved in October 2001, and which took effect on 1 January 2002, includes some parts of the local draft. It allocates the province 80% of revenue from forestry and fisheries and 70% from oil, gas and mining, provides for a Papua People's Council to protect the rights of indigenous inhabitants, and confirms the change of name to Papua.[59] Nevertheless, the PDP's Theys Hiu Eluay rejected the new legislation.[60]

In early 2002, the prognosis for resolving the Papuan conflict was poor. On the one hand, the autonomy law seemed unlikely to assuage pro-independence sentiment, while on the other there was no sign that OPM could achieve more than pin-prick successes in the face of Jakarta's increasingly hard-line military posture. Despite sympathy from small Melanesian states such as Nauru and Vanuatu and within PNG, and a campaign by NGOs in Western countries for the UN to review its conduct during the 1969 Act of Free Choice, there was no substantial international support for Papua's separation. The PNG government refused to provide sanctuary for OPM fighters. Moreover, tribal factionalism continued to undermine the independence movement. Although PDP leaders and Indonesian NGO activists called for dialogue, there seemed little chance of compromise by either Megawati's government or OPM. A possible concession from Jakarta might see Indonesia's government agreeing to regular talks with the PDP on the basis that independence remained only a long-term possibility.[61] However, the murder in November 2001 of Theys Hiu Eluay, blamed on the TNI, and escalating anti-Christian militia activity did not bode well for a peaceful settlement.[62]

The TNI and the secessionist provinces

The course of the Acehnese and Papuan conflicts is bound up with the development of relations between Indonesia's government and the armed forces, and with the closely-related efforts to reform Indonesia's security sector. The TNI's clear determination to impose hard-line solutions in Aceh and Papua has reinforced concerns that the military sees these and other peripheral conflicts as 'projects', where 'money is made, reputations are built and promotions gained'.[63] The conflicts in Aceh, Papua and elsewhere have helped to maintain the TNI's residual political influence in Jakarta – as it could 'portray itself as the only force capable of preventing the disintegration of Indonesia' while simultaneously undermining democratic reforms.[64]

These conflicts also justified the retention of the army's territorial system – the basis for the TNI's political influence and economic involvement outside Jakarta – and appeared to justify TNI efforts to take back control over internal-security operations from the police. Moreover, while the military's commercial activities are widespread throughout Indonesia, the lack of effective law and order in Aceh, Papua and other conflict-ridden provinces offers particularly good opportunities for profit. In Aceh, the TNI derives substantial financial benefits from Pertamina, and indirectly from ExxonMobil, for protecting the Arun oil and gas field. Military elements in Aceh have also allegedly profited from illegal logging, from growing and trafficking in marijuana and from extortion at roadblocks.[65] In Papua, Freeport has paid the TNI roughly $11m annually to protect its mining operation.[66]

The armed forces have had both political and economic reasons for prolonging the conflicts in Aceh and Papua. Military officers appeared to sabotage efforts by Habibie and Abdurrahman to contain the violence and seek negotiated settlements.[67] It has been alleged that TNI elements have helped sustain GAM, notably through the supply of weapons. At the same time, TNI officers may have sponsored a 'third force' masquerading as GAM guerrillas in order to justify a tougher military response.[68] Similarly, in Papua the TNI has allegedly armed and manipulated OPM factions responsible for kidnappings, as well as supposedly pro-independence militias which attacked police stations and other targets in late 2000. Some sources even claim that the TNI set up Satgas Papua in order to discredit the independence movement.[69]

Given this context, it is unlikely that measures such as special autonomy and dialogue can bring peace to Aceh and Papua in the absence of considerable further progress in strengthening civilian control over the TNI and reforming the security sector to ensure a halt to counter-productive abuses. The prosecution of TNI personnel for past abuses would be necessary as part of an effective settlement in either province.

Map 5 Riau

Wider secessionism?

Since the resolution of the East Timor problem in 1999, armed separatist struggles have been confined to Aceh and Papua. However, the more open political atmosphere throughout Indonesia since 1998 has allowed the expression of secessionist sentiment in other provinces.

Such secessionist calls have been loudest in Riau. The province includes Indonesia's most important oil fields and major forest resources in Sumatra, large natural-gas fields around the Natuna Islands, and prosperous industrial zones on the islands of Batam and Bintan, close to Singapore. Despite Riau's economic significance (its oil production alone is valued at 14% of national

GDP), nearly half of its population of three million lives in poverty. By early 2000, local activists' demands ranged from special autonomy to federalism or even full independence. Disturbances in Riau in 2000 and 2001 saw blockades of oil fields and tourist resorts, anti-Chinese riots and attacks on migrants from other provinces. But although secessionist propaganda claimed that 50,000 Riau citizens had undergone military training, and a group calling itself the Free Riau Forces attempted to mobilise popular opposition to Jakarta's rule, there was no evidence of an active armed independence movement, and the unofficial Riau People's Congress emphasised its intention to fight for independence peacefully.[70]

As he struggled for political survival in early 2001, Abdurrahman raised the supposed threat of wider separatism, claiming that as many as six provinces, including Aceh, East Java, Madura and Riau, would secede if he was ousted.[71] However, although relations between Jakarta and many provinces were strained, at issue in most cases was the distribution of economic and political power *within* Indonesia, rather than the country's territorial integrity. In several provinces, though, sporadic secessionist calls derive largely from local Muslims' wish to implement *sharia* law, or from non-Muslims' aim to avoid this. One emerging secessionist issue which might pose problems for Jakarta in the future concerns West Timor. According to the TNI, a 'Greater Timor State' movement plans to detach from Indonesia with a view to uniting with East Timor.[72] However, the TNI may have invented or exaggerated this supposed independence movement to justify the suppression of local political dissent.

Regional autonomy

The fall of Suharto's highly centralised regime allowed a major policy initiative on the reform of centre–periphery relations. Although the negative experiences of the decolonisation era effectively ruled out serious consideration in Jakarta of a federal system, in May 1999 Habibie approved laws decentralising regional administration and finances. Law 22/1999 allowed for the election by regional parliaments of provincial governors and district heads, who would no longer be bureaucrats representing the central government. Jakarta would still be responsible for foreign affairs, defence, justice and monetary and fiscal affairs, as well as national economic planning and natural-resource conservation. However,

Indonesia's 300-plus administrative districts, known as *kabupaten* (regencies) and *kotamadya* (municipalities), would take over virtually all other public spheres, including health, education and public works. Under Law 25/1999, 'equalisation grants' including a proportion of revenues from natural-resource exploitation (15% from oil, 30% from natural gas and 80% from mining, forestry and fisheries) would replace existing central-government grants.[73] The priority was to redistribute revenue to aggrieved resource-rich areas, including Riau and East Kalimantan. In theory at least, these laws would transform Indonesia from one of the world's most centralised states to a highly decentralised system. By devolving authority to districts rather than the more symbolically important provinces, the new laws also aimed to avoid encouraging national disintegration.

Critics voiced a variety of concerns over the decentralisation programme. The most important were:

- the potentially negative impact on less well-endowed provinces, particularly parts of Java, East Nusa Tenggara (Flores, Sumba and West Timor), and West Nusa Tenggara (Lombok and Sumbawa), which stood to lose revenue;
- the absence of an adequate legal framework to govern relations between the central government, the provinces and the districts;
- the lack of democratic checks and balances on the newly-empowered districts, reflecting the widespread weakness of national political parties at the grass-roots;
- the districts' lack of administrative capacity, particularly officials sufficiently competent to exercise new powers and spend new resources effectively;
- the increased potential for corruption in newly-enriched local authorities and competition for the spoils of office amongst regional political and traditional élites;
- an inadequate assessment of districts' revenue needs in order to meet their new responsibilities, and the related danger that regional administrations and assemblies might impose excessive and ultimately counter-productive new taxes on Indonesian and foreign companies, encourage over-exploitation of natural resources and run up debts through international borrowing;
- the potential for the oppressive role of the TNI's territorial structure to limit regional freedoms;

- the danger that empowering the districts might boost regional 'ethno-nationalism', leading to preferential treatment for indigenous people at the expense of ethnic outsiders; and
- the fear that some regions could feel sufficiently prosperous to secede.

Although perhaps only 10% of districts were ready to assume their new roles, implementation commenced as planned on 1 January 2001. Within weeks, it became clear that Jakarta intended to revise the autonomy legislation, the shortcomings of which were glaring. Vice-President Megawati, for whom the unitary state was sacrosanct, was evidently particularly concerned that the centre should reclaim powers and resources, while imposing a hierarchy in which provinces would control the distribution of resources to districts.[74] Once president, Megawati continued to argue for revisions, claiming that Indonesia risked becoming 'the Balkans of the eastern hemisphere'.[75] Sudarsono Hardjosoekarto, the Ministry of Home Affairs' director-general for regional public administration, claimed that the regions were increasingly contradicting the unitary-state principle by becoming 'sovereign entities'.[76]

However, the risk of alienating the regions constrained the central government's impulse to roll back autonomy. In some provinces, the benefits of decentralisation rapidly became clear; in Riau, for example, the budget of the provincial and district administrations increased six-fold.[77] In January 2002, Megawati's dilemma was clear when she told a meeting of provincial governors and district heads that, despite the need for amendments intended 'to strengthen our national unity and the integrity of the unitary state', there was 'no intention whatsoever to reduce, cancel or scrap the Autonomy Laws'.[78] By this time, traditional rulers and *adat* (local customary law) were reasserting their power in many parts of Indonesia, and the devolution process had taken on a life of its own.[79]

Is Indonesia disintegrating?

In early 2002, relations between Jakarta and Indonesia's regions were still in flux. However, it was by no means evident that Indonesia's territorial cohesion would break down. Even the secession of Aceh and Papua was not necessarily inevitable. Indonesia's leadership was evidently willing to use the military (including locally-recruited anti-independence militias) to maintain national unity. Although the country's widespread internal-security problems had stretched Indonesia's military capacity, the withdrawal from East Timor in 1999 increased the TNI's ability to intervene elsewhere in the archipelago. During the 1950s, a much less well-equipped military overcame a wide range of major internal-security threats.

The fact that international attitudes towards Aceh and Irian Jaya are distinct from those which motivated intervention in East Timor in 1999 will assist Indonesia to hold on to these provinces. Securing such international support and neutralising possible sources of external backing for separatism were primary objectives of Abdurrahman's oft-criticised foreign policy, which involved frequent visits to foreign capitals. Partly as a result, foreign leaders, in the West and the Middle East as well as in South-east and East Asia, have repeatedly reaffirmed support for Indonesia's continued territorial integrity; external backing for provincial separatism has been virtually absent. While GAM may not be linked to al-Qaeda, the US-led 'war against terrorism' has further reduced the likelihood of government-level international sympathy for the Acehnese cause, even if pressure is likely to continue on Jakarta to limit human-rights abuse by the security forces.

It remains to be seen whether the provincial special autonomy granted to Aceh and Papua will ultimately satisfy their populations and substantially undermine support for local armed groups. Although instability and violence may continue in the short- to medium-term, in the longer term (perhaps after several years) special autonomy may reduce tensions. However, while local political élites are likely to benefit politically and materially from assuming more powerful roles in running their home provinces, it seems unlikely that resistance to Indonesian control will end without justice for direct and indirect victims of human-rights abuse, who constitute a large part of the population in each province.

The greater freedoms for political, cultural and religious expression and increased prosperity allowed by special autonomy could further boost separatist sentiment. While Indonesia might be able to use its military power to maintain control indefinitely, this could require a level of brutality and human-rights abuse unacceptable internationally. It is conceivable that Indonesia might allow referendums on independence in Aceh and/or Papua rather than risk losing vital Western trade, investment and aid. The consequence in either case could well be a vote for secession. Separation could, however, be as messy as it was in East Timor.

The consequences of the separation of Papua or Aceh for the rest of the Indonesia are hard to predict. Such a development would constitute a blow to any incumbent Indonesian government's credibility, and might be used by the TNI to justify a stronger role in government. At first glance, the likely economic impact would also seem considerable given the important natural resources of both provinces. However, the economic benefits for Jakarta of maintaining control of Aceh and Papua would be qualified by:

- the planned retention at provincial level of the bulk of revenues from natural resources following the implementation of special autonomy;
- the cost of military operations to maintain control;
- the costs of foreign investment lost because of the impact of the conflicts on Indonesia's 'country risk' status; and
- in Aceh's case, the province's declining economic importance. By 2000, two of six gas-liquefaction plants had been closed. It was anticipated that Aceh's natural-gas production would decline from an annual average of 11.3m tonnes in the late 1990s to 3m tonnes in 2010.[80]

There is widespread fear in Indonesian political and military circles that Aceh's secession might have a 'knock-on' effect elsewhere in the archipelago.[81] (This is deemed less likely in the case of Papua given its exceptional historical and cultural circumstances.) But even the loss of Aceh would not necessarily be disastrous for the unity of the rest of Indonesia. Specific local factors, notably cultural particularism, historical grievance and natural-resource wealth, have combined to motivate the independence struggles in both Papua and Aceh. Although there have been calls in other provinces for greater autonomy or even a federal solution, there is little evidence that strong local political movements or leaders have emerged that could gain sufficient support to challenge rule from Jakarta decisively.

Except in Aceh, Papua, and to a lesser extent Riau, independence does not figure prominently in provincial politics. In the 1999 elections, Golkar, the arch-centralist party of the Suharto regime, won considerably more DPR seats in eastern Indonesia than any of its rivals. In part, the dominance of a national political perspective may be due to the tight requirements of Law 2/1999, which stipulates that parties contending elections must have branches in at least half of Indonesia's provinces, and in half of the regions in each of these provinces.[82] However, even if parties explicitly promoting local interests were allowed to compete in elections, they would be more likely to press for autonomy, rather than separation. A sense of belonging to Indonesia may be stronger than is often assumed: a nationwide survey in mid-2001 found that 81% of interviewees identified themselves as 'Indonesian', and only 11% by ethnic or religious labels.[83]

Despite the evident drawbacks of administrative and fiscal decentralisation as implemented since January 2001, devolving power and finances promises to ease regions' grievances, while allowing them to assert their rights within the context of continued national unity, which most Indonesians apparently prefer. Provinces may ultimately emerge as more powerful units than originally envisaged in the 1999 legislation, particularly in regions such as Riau and South Sulawesi. Decentralisation has already encouraged parts of existing provinces to seek their own provincial status. North Maluku became a province in its own right in 1999, and was followed during 2000 by Banten (from West Java), Bangka-Belitung (from South Sumatra) and Gorontalo (from North Sulawesi). Another ten potential provinces await parliamentary and presidential approval.[84]

In spite of Megawati's efforts to impose order on the decentralisation project, and the widespread allergy to federalism among Jakarta's political and military élite, her predecessor Abdurrahman may not have been too wide of the mark when he referred in early 2000 to Indonesia's 'future of wide-ranging autonomy, a federalist future'.[85] However, a stable decentralised format for Indonesia may not be possible for several years. In the meantime, devolving political and economic power will be fraught with dangers, not least that it may stimulate communal and social conflict.

Chapter 3

Horizontal conflict: inter-communal violence and Islamic politics

Beyond Aceh and Papua, recent violence in Indonesia has had little to do with separatism and does not directly challenge the country's territorial integrity. Nevertheless, since 1998 it has sometimes appeared that what Indonesians call 'horizontal' conflict has threatened to unravel the country's complex ethnic and religious patchwork. In eastern Indonesia, there has been vicious inter-communal fighting. At the same time, tensions between observant Muslims seeking a more Islamic form of governance and moderate Muslims and non-Muslims who prefer the secular status quo have challenged social and political stability, with significant implications for national cohesion.

Some of the most important factors which effectively cemented Indonesia's diverse ethnic and religious communities together under Suharto – notably rapid economic growth and the role of the armed forces in suppressing political, ethnic, and religious dissent – have weakened considerably since 1998. Simultaneously, greater political freedom has allowed ethnic and religious communities freer rein to air grievances that built up under the New Order. In many cases, indigenous communities have strongly resented the economic and social impact of immigrants from other provinces. Before its end after three decades in August 2000, Jakarta's transmigration project settled almost 10m people from overcrowded regions, mainly Java, Bali and Madura, in less populated provinces, particularly in eastern Indonesia. And democratisation has allowed local traditional élites to re-emerge as contenders for provincial power, at the same time as decentralisation has heightened political competition for control of local natural resources, budgets and patronage. All these factors have contributed to outbreaks of violence.

There has been much speculation over the role of provocateurs, supposedly sponsored by political and military élite elements linked to Suharto and the New Order, in fanning the flames of provincial conflict. Although clear evidence has proved elusive, and local actors have almost certainly been far more important in first provoking most conflicts, in some cases outside influences, including the Java-based Laskar Jihad (Holy War Troops) militia, have intensified and prolonged disarray.

The widespread communal clashes since 1999 have had serious implications for Indonesia's political and economic health. By rendering parts of the country ungovernable, the violence has undermined democracy, lending a veneer of credibility to claims by conservative political forces that only strong government, including a politically powerful TNI, can hold Indonesia together. At the same time, chronic unrest has reinforced international perceptions of Indonesia as a high-risk environment for investors.

Maluku and North Maluku

The most serious communal violence has been in the Maluku (Moluccas) group, where large-scale bloodletting between Muslims and Christians since January 1999 has left as many as 10,000 people dead, and created 500,000 refugees in a population of 2.4m.[1] The conflict's two main loci have been on the small island of Ambon in central Maluku, and in northern Halmahera in North Maluku. In central Maluku, both Muslims and Christians have claimed that the other side in the conflict has secessionist intent. After Muslim forces gained the upper hand in mid-2000, Maluku Protestant leaders established the Maluku Sovereignty Front (FKM), and in December 2000 demanded independence for Ambon and surrounding islands.[2] However, separatism was not the conflict's driving force. Although the FKM's leader was arrested in April 2001, even the TNI dismissed Muslim claims regarding the supposed separatist threat.[3]

The roots of these conflicts lay essentially in local communal antagonisms. Because of colonial-era missionary activity, a large proportion of Maluku's population is Christian, and Maluku

Map 6 Ambon – Distribution of Muslim and Christian-held Settlements, February 2001, according to Laskar Jihad

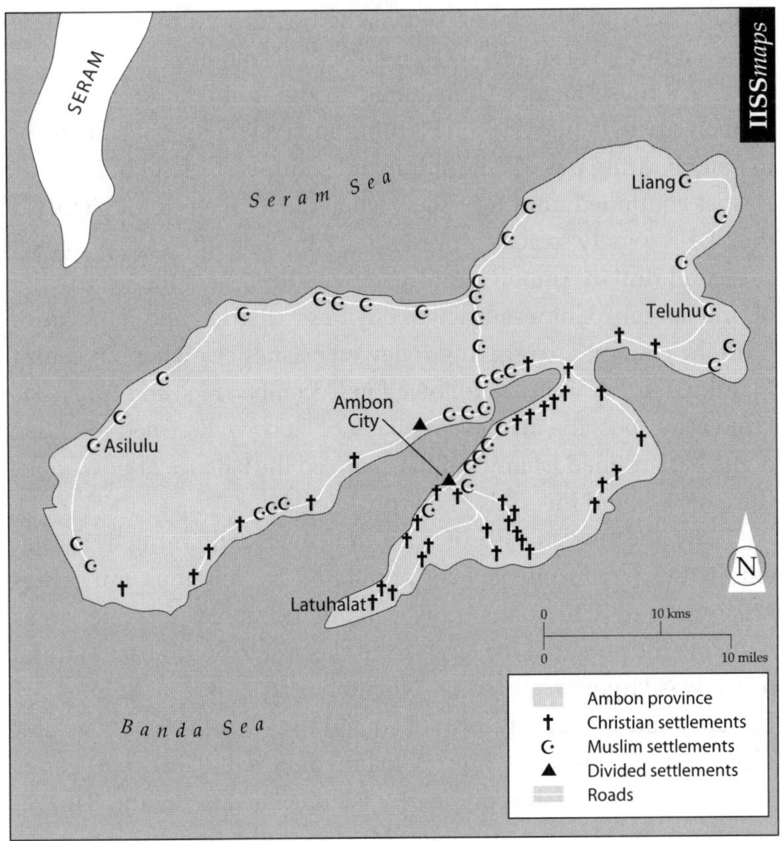

Source: Laskar Jihad website, www.laskerjihad.or.id

Protestants acted as administrators and soldiers throughout the Dutch East Indies. In 1971, there was an almost exact balance between Christians and Muslims in Maluku's population. However, because of government-sponsored and spontaneous in-migration and their higher birth-rate, by 1990 Muslims constituted 57% of the population.[4] Muslims increasingly dominated the provincial bureaucracy, holding three-quarters of the top 38 posts by 1999. Competition between unemployed Muslim and Christian youths for civil-service posts in Ambon city intensified, particularly with the regional economic crisis.[5] These and other social changes heightened inter-communal tensions. In the run-up to the June 1999 provincial elections, contending local élites attempted to use party politics as a route to bureaucratic power and control of patronage networks. In doing this, they exploited religious loyalties and communal gangs. Tension rose in December 1998, when a major Protestant gang, defeated in a Jakarta 'turf war', returned to Ambon.

All these factors contributed to the outbreak of conflict in Ambon city in January 1999.[6] Fighting spread widely, on Ambon and to neighbouring islands in central and south-east Maluku. Sporadic clashes continued until July 1999, when the local electoral victory of the PDI-P, widely seen as representing Christian interests, provoked a 'second riot' in Ambon city. The new fighting saw the destruction of the largely Chinese-owned business district and attacks on Catholic churches, triggering renewed clashes elsewhere in central Maluku. Further violence followed in December 1999 and June 2000. From May 2000, the arrival from Java of 6,000 well-armed members of the Laskar Jihad Islamic militia changed the balance of power, and Christians found themselves on the defensive.

By the second half of 2000, however, militant activity had eliminated territorial pockets populated by religious minorities; Muslims and Christians now largely occupied discrete areas, reducing the potential for large-scale clashes. In South-east Maluku, peace was largely restored by November 2000. But in Ambon city, Laskar Jihad repeatedly provoked fighting across the devastated urban centre between 'white' (Muslim) and 'red' (Christian) gangs. There were also clashes on nearby islands such as Seram, Saparua and Buru. In March 2001, 1,500 Muslim and Christian representatives met to discuss reconciliation, agreeing to use local traditions and customs to 'accommodate differences'.[7] Overall, the conflict abated appreciably during 2001, though an upsurge in bombings and shootings in November and December highlighted the potential for renewed hostilities. Government-sponsored peace talks in February 2002 resulted in the two sides agreeing to end their violence and surrender their weapons.[8] Renewed violence in April threatened to undermine this settlement, but also prompted the government to arrest the leaders of Laskar Jihad and the FKM. The government also vowed to expel Laskar Jihad's remaining forces from Maluku and to disband the FKM.[9] It seemed possible that the peace might hold.

Although not so widely reported, the conflict in North Maluku was even bloodier. It broke out in August 1999, after plans were announced for a new administrative district in northern Halmahera, populated by Muslim migrants from the island of Makian and including a newly-opened gold mine.[10] The clash occurred against the backdrop of North Maluku's imminent separation to form a new province, and of plans for provincial elections in June 2000. Competition for the spoils of office in this new unit was intense. Initial clashes between Protestants, backed by the Sultan of Ternate (as part of his rivalry with the neighbouring Sultan of Tidore) and Muslims in northern Halmahera left only small numbers dead. But in October–November 1999, all 8,000 Makian Muslims were expelled, provoking violence against Christians on the islands of Ternate and Tidore. The Sultan of Ternate used his 7,000-strong force of palace guards, including many Christians, against Muslim rioters, but at least 13,000 Christians were evacuated to North Sulawesi. In December 1999, Protestants in northern Halmahera retaliated, attacking villages populated by Muslim migrants and massacring hundreds. Attacks by the Ternate Sultan's guards on Muslims provoked intervention by the Sultanate of Tidore, and by the year's end the Sultan of Ternate was effectively defeated.[11]

The atrocities against Muslims in late 1999 precipitated revenge attacks on Protestants remaining in northern Halmahera by local militant Islamic groups and, from May 2000, by Laskar Jihad.[12] In one such attack in June, 4,000–5,000 Muslim fighters rampaged through a Christian settlement, killing more than 100 villagers. Soon afterwards, almost 500 Christian evacuees died when their overloaded vessel sank.[13] Following the expulsion of a large proportion of the Christian population, the North Maluku conflict's overall intensity diminished during 2000.[14] In February 2001, the provincial authorities began to repatriate refugees to their home villages. In May, Muslim and Christian residents in one sub-district held a traditional peace-making ceremony.[15]

A remarkable feature of the Maluku troubles was the Indonesian state's failure to restore order or provide security. During 1999, Jakarta politicians hardly focused on Maluku, being distracted by the economy's continuing problems, the June DPR elections, the East Timor crisis, and then the presidential election. Under both Habibie and Abdurrahman, the government evidently lacked ideas for resolving the conflict. As vice-president, Megawati was supposedly responsible for Maluku, but she displayed little interest, stopping for only two hours at the airport during her first visit to Ambon in December 1999.

Maluku's extensive archipelagaic geography, a lack of experience in dealing with communal conflict, poor leadership, inadequate command and control mechanisms, financial and logistical under-resourcing and the torn loyalties of both locally-recruited personnel and troops from other provinces – all conspired to reduce the security forces' effectiveness. A civil emergency, declared belatedly in June 2000, allowed Maluku's governor to use any necessary means (including preventive detention and curfew) to end the conflict, but he failed to coordinate an effective response involving the civilian authorities, police and TNI. The deployment of substantial military and police reinforcements, which brought security-force strength up to 21 battalions in Maluku and North Maluku, helped to contain the fighting. But although these forces imposed curfews and operated checkpoints, they seldom mounted effective, intelligence-led offensive operations against communal militias.[16]

Elements of the security forces often exacerbated the conflict. Military and police personnel not only sold weapons to militia groups, but also sometimes became directly engaged in the conflict. In August 1999 and January 2000, for example, witnesses accused Kostrad troops of helping Muslim militia to massacre Christian villagers. The security forces did nothing to stop several thousand Laskar Jihad militiamen travelling from Java to Maluku, or to prevent them from joining battle. In July 2000, troops in Ambon city were filmed providing covering fire to Muslim fighters.[17] Muslims, on the other hand, alleged that the police were biased towards Christians. After Laskar Jihad forces ransacked its Ambon headquarters in June 2000, the local Brimob unit disintegrated, with many personnel deserting to join militias. At best, there was little cooperation between the TNI and the police; at worst, their personnel sometimes fought each other.[18] The breakdown of the wider security-sector apparatus, including the effective absence of courts and prisons, further undermined law and order.[19]

The armed forces' performance in Maluku was not utterly disastrous, however. During 2000, the TNI deployed two specially-formed 'joint battalions', each comprising elements drawn from Kopassus, the marines and air force special forces. Their willingness to act against trouble-makers, which by that time usually meant

Muslims, soon provoked allegations from Laskar Jihad and related Islamic organisations that the joint battalions were biased and brutal.[20] However, they appeared to perform effectively, and probably helped to stabilise the conflict in central Maluku.

Religious and ethnic conflict beyond Maluku

Events in other parts of Indonesia have also demonstrated the incapacity of the state apparatus to cope effectively with communal conflict. Outside Maluku, the main site of Muslim–Christian strife has been in Central Sulawesi's Poso district. By early 2002, perhaps as many as 1,000 people had been killed and 80,000 displaced, out of a population of 300,000.[21] The sources of social tension were similar to Maluku's, particularly Muslim migrants' demographic and economic impact and political competition.[22] The Christian élite resented its exclusion from the top levels of the district administration following the June 1999 elections, as these posts not only controlled the allocation of public-works contracts, but also stood to gain control of more substantial revenues after decentralisation. As in Maluku, in the conflict's early stages local faction leaders attempted to exploit communal loyalties, but the fighting soon spiralled out of control.[23]

Since 1998, there have been four main bouts of conflict in Poso:

- an initial round of fighting and arson started by drunken youths, but controlled by local officials, in December 1998;
- a second eruption of violence following another minor incident in April 2000, resulting in the expulsion of Christians from Poso town;
- revenge attacks by Christians against Muslim villages in May–June 2000, including an attack on a mosque in which almost 200 Muslims were killed; and
- 'Poso 4' in November–December 2001, mainly involving attacks on Christian villages by Muslim forces including Laskar Jihad militiamen, between 500 and 1,000 of whom had arrived since August.

The religious 'cleansing' of Poso town in the second round of fighting resulted in the district population's segregation between 'red' and 'white' zones, with the town of Tentena becoming the headquarters of what amounted to a Christian mini-state.[24] As in Maluku, the government and security forces displayed remarkable ineptitude. Their failure to respond effectively to the Christians' expulsion contributed directly to the subsequent retaliation against Muslims. In the absence of judicial measures against Muslim leaders, the subsequent sentencing of three Christian gang leaders to death for their part in the mosque atrocity helped provoke 'Poso 4'.[25]

Police inaction at every stage until late 2001 allowed the conflict to escalate, while TNI troops sometimes joined the fighting on the Muslim side.[26] Security-force personnel allegedly profited from selling arms to militias, as well as from controlling roadblocks.[27] As was the case elsewhere, the TNI and the police were unable to work effectively with each other or the local authorities.[28] Even the arrival of Laskar Jihad forces failed to provoke an official response at national or provincial level. Only after the fourth round of fighting did Jakarta deploy sufficient troops and police to begin managing the problem.[29] Although even then the government did not declare a civil emergency, this more decisive action seemed to create better conditions for negotiation and, in late December 2001, a fifth round of peace talks involving Muslim and Christian representatives concluded with a ten-point settlement. In this 'Malino Declaration', the factions agreed to end violence and reject interference by outsiders (a reference to Laskar Jihad).[30]

There have also been serious communal disturbances in two of Kalimantan's four provinces, where local (and possibly national) political forces have exploited tensions between the indigenous Dayaks and Malays and mainly Madurese immigrants. That the Dayaks are mainly Christian or animist while the Madurese are Muslim widened the gulf between them, but was not the root of the problem: many local Muslim Malays also resented the migrants. In December 1996, even before the New Order's collapse, large-scale fighting erupted between Dayaks and Madurese close to West Kalimantan's provincial capital, Pontianak. This outbreak was notable for its savagery: approximately 500 people – mostly Madurese – are believed to have died.[31] As in subsequent pogroms, the Dayaks frequently beheaded their victims. Tough measures by the army and police suppressed the conflict by March 1997, but the government made little effort to promote durable reconciliation

Map 7 Kalimantan

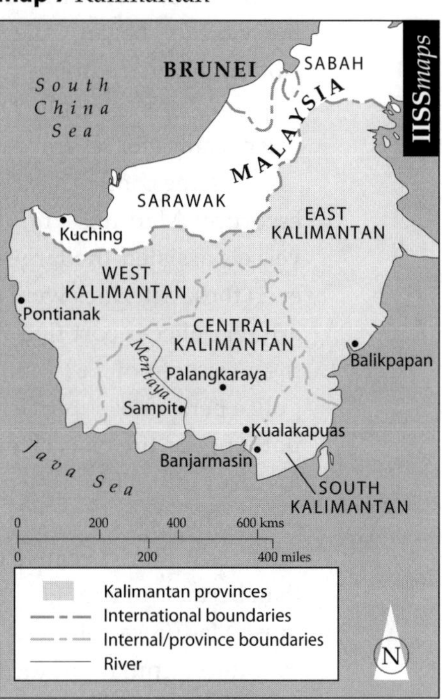

between the communities. In February and March 1999, Malays and Dayaks clashed with Madurese in Sambas district, also in West Kalimantan; as many as 3,000 may have died, though the official death toll was 260. Thousands of Madurese fled to Pontianak, where resentment amongst local Dayaks and Malays has subsequently simmered, sometimes boiling over into violence.[32]

Violence in neighbouring Central Kalimantan in February 2001 was even more serious, and affected all major towns in the province's south. This anti-Madurese pogrom took place against the background of the decentralisation programme, which had heightened ethnic consciousness amongst the Dayaks. Indigenous local officials may have provoked the initial attacks, and a senior Dayak academic was eventually arrested for encouraging anti-Madurese violence.[33] These attacks began in a district capital, Sampit, and spread during the following month to the provincial capital, Palangkaraya, and the towns of Pangkalanbun and Kualakapuas. At least 2,000 people were reported killed during the first two weeks alone, and most remaining Madurese (80,000–90,000 people) were evacuated, mainly to Madura and East Java.[34]

As in Maluku and Poso, the response of the government and security forces to the Central Kalimantan disturbances was slow, inadequate and uncoordinated. Abdurrahman was out of the country at the time, and refused to return prematurely. During the first week, the security forces largely stood aside while Dayak gangs slaughtered large numbers of Madurese. In part this was because the police were ill-equipped and ill-trained for non-lethal riot control. The army was apparently interested in showing that the police were unable to cope, and was able to justify its own inaction by referring to the allocation of roles agreed when the police separated from the armed forces in 1999. Local commanders' complacency, together with poor coordination between TNI headquarters and the local command, compounded these problems, so that army reinforcements only arrived a week after the violence began. Alleged efforts by senior officers to discredit Abdurrahman's administration may also have contributed to the slow response.[35] As a result, Dayak gangs were able to take control of Palangkaraya for several days, terrorising and expelling local Madurese.

In the conflict's early stages, the security forces' main role was escorting Madurese refugees to places of relative safety. Naval vessels assisted the large-scale evacuation of refugees to Java, but even these activities were conducted ineptly. In one incident, a well-armed police escort fled when faced by a Dayak gang, resulting in the massacre of 118 Madurese. In a separate incident, army and police personnel supervising the exodus of Madurese from Sampit's port opened fire on each other, apparently in a dispute over the right to extort bribes from the refugees.[36]

The Central Kalimantan conflict had largely died down by May 2001, more because the Dayaks had achieved their objectives than because of firm government action. There was little chance that most Madurese refugees could return and, as part of its conflict-resolution 'initiative' for the province, Jakarta announced that all 'sacred' lands would be returned to the indigenous people.[37] Although separatism had not motivated the clashes and there was no evidence of any organised Dayak independence movement, at the root of Jakarta's evident wish to appease the Dayaks may have been a concern to pre-empt this 'horizontal' conflict from transmuting into a secessionist movement involving a challenge from indigenous people across Kalimantan.[38]

Since the late 1990s, there have also been relatively minor outbreaks of communal violence elsewhere. However, most areas of the country have been unaffected. In a number of highly heterogeneous provinces – notably North Sulawesi, East Kalimantan and South Kalimantan – local government, police, military and religious leaders have helped to keep tensions from escalating, demonstrating that measures ranging from greater police vigilance to dialogue between potential adversaries can help to forestall conflict.[39]

The challenge of Islamic radicalism

Since the relaxation of political constraints in 1998, Muslim political movements have proliferated and expanded, and some have challenged the secular basis of Indonesia's statehood. Under Sukarno, the Pancasila ('five principles': monotheism, humanitarianism, nationalism, popular sovereignty and social justice) were entrenched as the state philosophy, effectively eclipsing the alternative vision of Indonesia as an Islamic state, or even as a state where Muslims were subject to *sharia* law. Despite the assistance rendered by Muslim organisations in eliminating Indonesia's political left in the 1960s, during the 1970s and 1980s Suharto's New Order attempted to depoliticise Indonesian Islam. In 1973, the four surviving Muslim political parties were forced to combine as the PPP, which was subsequently made to accept the Pancasila as its only ideology. The armed forces did not hesitate to use force to control dissident Muslims.

Indonesian Islam has never constituted a unified or homogeneous social or political force. Until the 1980s, most rural Muslims in Java belonged to the syncretic *abangan* tradition, which is influenced by animist and Hindu values, as well as Islam. This flexible outlook, tolerant of diverse religious beliefs and practices, is reflected in the Pancasila. Nevertheless, under the New Order large numbers of Indonesian Muslims became more strictly observant in their religious practices, largely in reaction to urbanisation, materialism and other forms of modernisation associated with rapid economic development. In Java, this trend is referred to as *santrinisation*, the strengthening of the *santri* or devout tradition. From the late 1980s, Suharto attempted to harness Indonesian Islam's growing strength to compensate for weakening support for his presidency from the armed forces. In 1990, he encouraged the establishment of ICMI, and during the 1990s observant Muslims became more prominent in the political mainstream.

Since 1998, political Islam has been liberated from its role as an instrument of the New Order, and Islamic issues have become central to the political debate in Jakarta. Most Indonesian Muslims still belong to or support one of two mass social movements: NU and Muhammadiyah, which together claim a following of 50–70m. NU's outlook is traditionalist, in the sense of tolerating a degree of religious syncretism, and it draws support primarily from rural east and central Java; Muhammadiyah is a modernist movement favouring stricter religious observance, and finding support in towns and cities across Indonesia. In terms of party affiliation, NU supporters generally adhere to either the PKB or PPP; Muhammadiyah is linked with PAN. Despite their Islamic precepts,

NU and Muhammadiyah both support the idea of a secular state, are essentially tolerant in their stance towards non-Muslims and have constituted pillars of Indonesia's emerging civil society since 1998.

More radical Islamic politicians have argued, however, that *sharia* law should be enforced on all Muslims, which would be achieved by inserting the 'Jakarta Charter', obliging all 'adherents of Islam to carry out Islamic law', into the constitution. Vice-President Hamzah Haz's PPP, the PBB and the PK, along with various vociferous extra-parliamentary groups, notably the Defenders of Islam Front (FPI) and the Indonesian Holy Warriors' Assembly (MMI), support this idea. However, there is no groundswell of opinion in favour of *sharia* law among the general Muslim population, and there was insufficient parliamentary support for its inclusion in the debate on constitutional revisions during the 2000 and 2001 MPR sessions. Muhammadiyah and NU have both made clear their opposition to the Jakarta Charter.[40]

Sharia law is unlikely to be adopted in the foreseeable future and, even if it was, would only directly affect Muslims. Nevertheless, the prospect has alarmed Indonesia's non-Muslims, who fear the erosion of the secular constitution. Non-Muslims have registered their concern particularly dramatically in eastern Indonesia. In August 2000, the heads of the 14 districts of East Nusa Tenggara province (which includes West Timor and Flores) threatened to establish a breakaway Republic of Eastern Indonesia if the Jakarta Charter was adopted.[41] In North Sulawesi, a congress of the Christian Minahasa people delivered an ultimatum to the MPR claiming that the Jakarta Charter's insertion into the constitution would result in the secession of the district that they dominate.[42] Conversely, in some Muslim-dominated parts of Indonesia local support for an Islamicised legal system is much stronger than at the centre. In South Sulawesi, for instance, Muslim groups have threatened to secede from Indonesia if Jakarta does not permit a form of special autonomy that would allow implementation of *sharia* law. During 2002, activists encouraged by the prominence of *sharia* in Aceh's autonomy package pressed for its adoption in West Java, Banten, West Sumatra and West Kalimantan. In places, newly autonomous districts exceeded their allotted powers to enforce Islamic rules.[43]

More radically, there is also a movement supporting the establishment of an Islamic state. The main force of this movement is

Laskar Sabilah, a 100,000-strong militia based in west and central Java and south Sumatra. Another body campaigning for an Islamic state is Jemaah Islamiah (Islamic Assembly). Other groups, such as Hizb al-Thahrir (Party of Liberation), support the re-establishment of a universal Islamic caliphate.[44]

Most Muslim parties and organisations are linked to *laskar* groups, membership of which has expanded dramatically since 1998. Given sufficient funding, militias find little difficulty in recruiting from the ever-growing pool of unemployed young people and gangs linked to organised crime, as well as from among committed zealots. Laskar Jihad has interfered directly in Ambon, North Maluku and Poso, and in early 2002 sent personnel to Papua to train anti-independence militias.[45] Laskar Pembela Islam, the FPI's militia, has conducted 'sweeps' in Javanese cities, aimed at disrupting gambling dens, bars, discos and red-light areas. After the US and UK struck at Taliban and al-Qaeda forces in Afghanistan in October 2001, FPI leader Habib Rizieq Shihab threatened to 'sweep' Indonesia of American and British nationals. Like Laskar Jihad, the FPI is allegedly linked to TNI elements, which apparently see these groups as useful for simultaneously balancing the left, highlighting the dangers of Islamic extremism, undermining the civilian government and, in the case of Laskar Jihad, fighting separatism.[46] However, while these groups may have benefited from military backing, their political leaders have their own agendas and are by no means simply puppets controlled by the TNI. Those groups seeking an Islamic state and the militias associated with MMI (such as Laskar Jundullah) are largely outside the influence of the TNI, which regards them as serious threats to political stability.

Groups such as Laskar Jihad, FPI and MMI have achieved a far higher political profile than their popularity warrants, and radicalism remains on the fringes of Indonesian Islam. Although there has been considerable militant activism in support of the Jakarta Charter, imposing *sharia* law remains a minority cause. Opposition among younger PPP members to the Jakarta Charter was one reason for a split in the party, with the PPP Reformasi faction breaking away in January 2002.[47] An Islamic republic is an even less popular proposition. NU and Muhammadiyah continue to moderate the outlook and behaviour of most Indonesian Muslims. Many young Indonesians are liberal in their social outlook, and show little interest in fulfilling religious obligations.

The TNI remains a significant obstacle to any tampering with Indonesia's secular state. At the same time, radical Islam is divided between numerous organisations, and seeks diverse objectives.[48]

In the longer term, though, Islamic radicalism could damage Indonesia's stability and national cohesion. Long-term economic hardship could further reinforce widespread popular disillusionment with a mainstream political élite increasingly seen as ineffective, factionalised, corrupt and self-seeking. Anti-Western sentiment has grown as a result of the US-led war in Afghanistan and the Palestinian crisis of early 2002, and may further undermine mainstream political leaders' legitimacy unless they distance themselves from the West. Moreover, the *sharia* issue is unlikely to disappear as Muslim leaders and parties canvass support in advance of the 2004 elections. In early 2002, Vice-President Hamzah was apparently building political alliances with the leaders of Laskar Jihad, FPI and MMI.[49] As a likely presidential candidate in 2004, PAN leader Amien Rais will need support from smaller Muslim parties, and may find it difficult to disavow the idea of amending the constitution to accommodate the Jakarta Charter.[50] If Indonesia appeared to be heading towards a regime that would accommodate observant Muslims' interests more fully, non-Muslims would almost certainly become more politically assertive. But because of the widespread intermingling of religious communities, even in those areas where non-Muslims predominate, the most likely outcome would be not the clear-cut separation of provinces from Indonesia, but more widespread, chronic civil strife.

Disintegration from the centre?

Although local social developments help to explain communal conflict in Maluku, Poso, Kalimantan and elsewhere, such violence could not have occurred if successive central governments had been stronger and more competent. Civilian leaders were responsible for some contributory factors, notably the impact of decentralisation on local communal relations. But the security forces did not act sufficiently quickly or decisively to prevent ethnic and religious conflict from escalating. The military acquiesced in the intervention of Laskar Jihad in eastern Indonesian conflicts, and with the police often became directly involved in supporting communal factions. Together, civilian politicians and the security forces allowed local disputes to spiral out of control. While communal conflicts had become generally less intense by early 2002, this was due as much to contending factions achieving their objectives as to the success of Jakarta's belated efforts at resolution.

Economic difficulties, the weakness of political institutions and civil society, and shortcomings in the security forces will almost certainly combine to ensure that conflict between ethnic and religious communities continues to plague Indonesia. While the country's movement towards a quasi-federalist structure by way of decentralisation and special-autonomy arrangements may help Jakarta to keep provinces such as Aceh and Riau inside Indonesia, it may also exacerbate conflicts elsewhere. In the longer term, *santrinisation* and shifts in the balance of political forces at the centre may exacerbate such 'horizontal' problems, which could ultimately pose more serious challenges to Indonesia's national cohesion, the interests of foreign investors and regional security than the more high-profile 'vertical' conflicts in Aceh and Papua.

Chapter 4

Regional and international implications of Indonesia's disarray

Since 1998, the wider ramifications of Indonesia's turmoil have prompted considerable concern in South-east Asia, Australia, Japan and the West. There is worry not only over security issues that are already apparent, but also over the potential consequences of further deterioration in Indonesia's economic, social and political condition and, in the worst case, the country's disintegration. Prominent among other governments' security concerns are anxieties over the changing orientation of Indonesia's foreign policy and its strategic ramifications, contagious political radicalism, international terrorist links to Indonesia's Islamic militants, large-scale unregulated population movements, piracy and environmental dangers. However, external military intervention remains unlikely except in the worst case scenario of Indonesia's disintegration.

Indonesia's foreign policy in the region and beyond

The Suharto regime was viewed positively in the West and non-communist South-east Asia partly because of its generally restrained and constructive foreign policy. Although a leading non-aligned nation, Indonesia was at the same time essentially and reliably pro-Western. Diplomatic relations with China were suspended until 1990 and, even then, Indonesia remained suspicious of Beijing's role in South-east Asia. In 1995, Jakarta even entered into a bilateral consultative security agreement with Australia. The Agreement on Maintaining Security (AMS) indicated that Australia's long-standing fears of an 'Indonesian threat' – often defined in terms of possible aggression against PNG or even military incursions into northern Australia – had been laid to rest. Canberra now saw Indonesia as a strategic barrier to threats from further north, particularly an increasingly powerful and assertive China.

Suharto's New Order also had a crucial impact on Indonesia's foreign policy in its immediate region. Between the late 1950s and the mid-1960s, Sukarno exported instability through policies of Confrontation against West New Guinea, and then Malaysia. After Suharto seized power, Confrontation was wound down. Indonesia's new posture allowed a process of reconciliation within the region that was cemented with the formation in 1967 of the Association of South-east Asian Nations (ASEAN), which became the cornerstone of Suharto's foreign policy. Within ASEAN, Indonesia was accepted as first amongst equals and acted as a low-key regional leader. This constructive role bolstered the wider international credibility of Indonesia's diplomacy.

The Indonesian armed forces, and Suharto himself, exerted crucial influence over the structure and practice of Indonesia's foreign policy between the late 1960s and the late 1990s, ensuring continuity and predictability. There were hints of change during the 1990s, as the military's political role declined and Muslim politicians assumed greater influence. The end of the Cold War generated some tensions in relations with the West, particularly over East Timor and human rights more generally. But overall, Western and ASEAN governments still viewed Indonesia in extremely positive terms. There was widespread hope in the region and beyond that Indonesia's inevitable political transition would be gradual, avoiding a radical nationalist or Islamic takeover. Governments well-disposed towards Suharto generally hoped that he would eventually be succeeded by another conservative, secular, development-oriented general, who would ensure continuity in Indonesia's foreign as well as domestic policies.

In the event, Indonesia's political transition was anything but gradual, and the country's international outlook has changed significantly since Suharto was ousted. For the first year and a half after May 1998, foreign policy remained more-or-less recognisable under long-serving Foreign Minister Ali Alatas. But this period also saw strains emerge in relations with both regional neighbours and Western states. These became much more apparent under

Abdurrahman. Beyond a vague intention of restoring a greater independence to Indonesia's foreign relations, manifested in efforts to cement closer ties in the Middle East and with China, it was hard to discern any clear underlying principle in Abdurrahman's international outlook. While his frequent foreign trips may have bolstered international support for Indonesia's national cohesion, they did not lend substance to its foreign policy.

Indonesia's turmoil has seriously affected its bilateral relations in South-east Asia, as well as ASEAN's coherence and standing. The economic and political crisis of 1998–99 damaged Indonesia's ties with Singapore, previously its closest collaborator within the Association. Despite Singapore's announcement in January 2000 of a plan to assist Indonesia's economic recovery, there was another dip in bilateral relations the following November, when Abdurrahman took the city-state to task for a range of apparent shortcomings in its foreign policy.[1] He even suggested that Indonesia was disillusioned with ASEAN and interested in setting up an alternative regional organisation, the West Pacific Forum, grouping Indonesia with Australia, New Zealand, PNG, East Timor and possibly the Philippines.[2] The idea surfaced again during talks between Abdurrahman and Australian Prime Minister John Howard in June 2001.[3]

After Megawati replaced Abdurrahman in July 2001, she visited all nine other ASEAN members to emphasise the Association's centrality in her government's foreign-policy outlook. However, the new foreign minister, Hassan Wirayuda, pointed out that ASEAN's larger members, including Indonesia, would need to overcome their domestic problems before the Association could launch new initiatives.[4] Although Megawati spoke of restoring Indonesia's 'big brother' role in ASEAN, this remained unrealistic as long as the country was plagued by economic stagnation and political violence.[5] Indonesia's requests for selective exemptions from tariff cuts were a significant factor slowing progress towards establishing the ASEAN Free Trade Area (AFTA), which had by the late 1990s become the grouping's showpiece initiative.[6]

Indonesia's foreign policy towards the West has also been affected. The 1999 East Timor crisis, and particularly Australia's role in it, accentuated the anti-Western sentiment reawakened by the financial crisis. One immediate casualty in 1999 was the AMS, which

Jakarta revoked. An embargo on military-to-military links and the supply of military equipment, imposed by the US during the East Timor violence in 1999, has further reinforced anti-Western feeling. Many Indonesian politicians and TNI officers believe that Western governments, particularly the US and Australia, are conspiring to undermine Indonesia's unity, for example by supporting 'Christian' secessionist movements in Irian Jaya and Maluku. Although Indonesia's relations with Western states stabilised after Megawati became president, within months the issue of terrorism imposed new strains.

By contrast, China's regional posture since the late 1990s has reaped diplomatic benefits in Indonesia, as in other parts of South-east Asia. By not devaluing its currency during the financial crisis, which could have further damaged the already devastated Indonesian economy, China sowed goodwill. This was in apparent contrast to the economic cures imposed by the West, which appeared to discount the costs of social distress. Significantly, Beijing's response to savage attacks by rioters on local ethnic Chinese in Jakarta in May 1998 was belated and low-key.[7] These developments set the scene for a notable warming in Beijing's relations with Indonesia, and for Jakarta to put aside (if not totally abandon) concerns about China as a security threat. There are, however, limits to this Sino-Indonesian *rapprochement*, and there remains much more substance in Indonesia's relations with the West. Indonesia still depends on Western and Japanese trade, investment and aid, as well as financial assistance from Western-dominated institutions. Competition rather than collaboration characterises Indonesia's economic relations with China, and senior TNI officers are likely to remain suspicious of China's long-term intentions. Nevertheless, Indonesia's warmer relations with China may have important strategic implications, such as further eroding ASEAN's ability to present a united diplomatic front in the event of renewed Chinese pressure on its members' territorial claims in the South China Sea.

Political contagion

Since the late 1990s, some South-east Asian governments have feared that Indonesia's separatist and communal conflicts might spill over into their countries. In particular, the regional example that might be created by provinces breaking free from Indonesia concerns the

Philippines and Thailand, which face Muslim separatist challenges in their respective southern regions of Mindanao and Pattani. The Moro Islamic Liberation Front (MILF) in Mindanao explicitly identified East Timor's independence referendum as a precedent, and in November 1999 the Philippines' foreign secretary expressed fears of 'a disease of separatist turmoil' sweeping the region if Aceh won independence.[8] These fears have prompted ASEAN members to reaffirm their collective support for Indonesia's national cohesion and territorial integrity.[9]

Malaysia, ruled by a formally democratic but effectively semi-authoritarian coalition, is closely linked to Indonesia by ties of language, religion and culture, as well as geographical proximity. Thus, its concerns over Indonesia's political evolution are deeper and broader than those in Thailand and the Philippines. In late 1998, supporters of dismissed and subsequently imprisoned former Deputy Prime Minister Anwar Ibrahim adopted anti-Suharto activists' slogan of *reformasi* (reform) as their own. Indonesia's new political plurality, and the increased prominence of Islamic politics there, threatened to destabilise Malaysia's political system to the advantage of the Islamic Party of Malaysia and other opposition groups. In late 1999, one Malaysian commentator compared the potentially destabilising regional impact of Indonesia's democratisation with the effect of the French revolution on early nineteenth century Europe.[10] Although in November 2000 Abdurrahman pledged to respect ASEAN's non-interference principle, the Malaysian authorities remained concerned over the support anti-government groups received from Indonesian sympathisers, and particularly that mass demonstrations and political violence, so common in Indonesia from 1998, could spread to Malaysia.[11] The Malaysian government also worried about Indonesia's potential 'Balkanisation', which Defence Minister Najib Tun Razak described in February 2001 as the greatest security threat in South-east Asia. A specific concern was that increasing agitation amongst indigenous Dayaks in Indonesian Kalimantan might spread into Sabah and Sarawak, Malaysia's Borneo states.[12]

International terrorism

Despite the concerns of its neighbours, until recently it seemed that post-Suharto Indonesia was a net importer of political extremism and violence. During 2001, for instance, Malaysian Muslim militants allegedly joined the communal fighting in Ambon, and helped in a series of bombings in Jakarta.[13] The illicit trade in light weapons from Thailand to Aceh and from the Philippines to Maluku was widely reported, as was non-governmental Malaysian support for GAM.[14]

Since the beginning of September 2001, a more complex picture has emerged. Following a number of arrests earlier in the year of alleged Islamic terrorists in Malaysia, Malaysian Prime Minister Mahathir Mohamad claimed that militants were planning to establish a 'Sovereign Islamic Archipelago', including Malaysia, Muslim-populated parts of Indonesia and the southern Philippines.[15] By that time, Washington was expressing concern over growing al-Qaeda-related activity in Indonesia.[16] In July, a suspected al-Qaeda team from Yemen arrived in Jakarta on a mission to attack the US embassy, but fled after becoming aware of an Indonesian surveillance operation. It later emerged that, before 11 September, US intelligence agencies had anticipated that the next major attack by al-Qaeda would be on US interests in South-east Asia.

After 11 September, South-east Asia rapidly emerged as a 'second front' in the US-led struggle against the al-Qaeda network. There was tentative evidence that hijackers in the US attacks had held meetings in Malaysia, and of other links between al-Qaeda and Islamic militants in regional countries including Indonesia where, rumours hinted, Osama bin Laden had already or might soon take refuge. Some South-east Asian governments responded quickly to US calls for cooperation. Manila agreed to the US sending troops to the southern Philippines to exercise with its forces operating against the Abu Sayyaf group. Singapore provided logistical support for increased numbers of transiting US military aircraft and ships, and Malaysia promised full collaboration.

Megawati met US President George W. Bush in Washington just a week after 11 September and, with the incentive of $650m in US economic assistance, promised Indonesia's assistance against terrorism.[17] However, it was soon evident that Megawati's need to appease domestic Muslim political forces, inside as well as outside her government, as well as resistance from elements of the TNI, would make it difficult for Jakarta to cooperate as fully as Washington might have wished. Even before the US attacked Afghanistan, the FPI and other militant groups began a campaign of anti-American demonstrations and intimidation of US businesses and citizens, forcing the US embassy's temporary closure. In October, the beginning of the war in Afghanistan led some religious leaders to call for the suspension of diplomatic ties with Washington.[18] Responding to concern over the war amongst even moderate Muslims, Megawati requested that the US limit its military operations.[19] Vice-President Hamzah, who had earlier claimed that the 11 September attacks would 'cleanse the US of its sins', demanded that the war cease.[20] Although it curbed anti-US demonstrations, banned Indonesians from travelling to Afghanistan to fight US forces, and claimed readiness to take strong action if concrete evidence connected Indonesians to international terrorism, Megawati's administration failed to act firmly against Indonesian radicals linked to terrorist suspects elsewhere in the region, and repeatedly cast doubt on their alleged links to al-Qaeda.[21]

In November 2001, US Deputy Secretary of Defense Paul Wolfowitz warned that Indonesia was 'wide open' to infiltration by al-Qaeda.[22] By early 2002, it seemed increasingly clear that terrorist groups linked to al-Qaeda had been using Indonesia as their South-east Asian base, and that Indonesians probably commanded the regional terrorist network. In January, Singapore's government announced that its Internal Security Department had arrested 15 suspects (mainly local Muslims) in connection with a plot to attack US, British, Australian and Israeli targets in the city-state.[23] Most of those arrested belonged to the local branch of the Indonesian-based group Jemaah Islamiah, which was allegedly aligned with al-Qaeda. In mid-January, the Philippine police arrested five suspected Jemaah Islamiah members including Fathur Rahman Al-Ghozi, an Indonesian suspected of acting as a regional intermediary for al-Qaeda, and seized explosives and weapons apparently intended for the Singaporean terrorists.[24] Evidence from the arrests in Malaysia and Singapore seemed to indicate that Indonesia's political disarray and lawlessness since the late 1990s had allowed al-Qaeda to develop close working links with the MMI and other local militant groups.[25] US and Indonesian intelligence also claimed that al-Qaeda had used a training camp in Central Sulawesi's Poso district.[26] Reports in early 2002 indicated that Jemaah Islamiah militants planned a long-term campaign in South-east Asia, with US interests in Indonesia as the most likely initial targets.[27] In February 2002, Admiral Dennis Blair, then commander-in-chief of US Pacific Command, told a

Congressional hearing of his concern over Jakarta's failure to arrest any terrorist suspects.[28]

International and domestic pressure on Megawati's government to take action had some effect in early 2002. In January, the Indonesian authorities covertly extradited a terrorist subject to Egypt with US assistance.[29] They also questioned – but did not arrest – Abu Bakar Bashir, leader of the MMI, amid growing evidence that he also directed both Malaysia's Mujahidin Group (KMM) and Jemaah Islamiah, and may have acted on behalf of al-Qaeda.[30] Further measures were aimed at tracking down a key Jemaah Islamiah suspect, Riduan Isamuddin, who was believed to have fled the country by mid-February. Jakarta intensified intelligence exchanges with Singapore, Malaysia, the Philippines, Pakistan, Australia and Interpol, as well as the US, and set up a task force to coordinate this cooperation. In May, Indonesia joined with Malaysia and the Philippines to sign an agreement covering 27 areas of cooperation against terrorism and other cross-border crime.[31] Intelligence from Indonesia helped the Philippines to arrest Agus Dwikarna, an important figure in Laskar Jundullah, which had allegedly operated the Poso camp for al-Qaeda. The government was also preparing new anti-terrorism legislation, although this met with resistance from human-rights activists, who feared its use to justify wider political repression.[32]

Jakarta's commitment to uprooting internationally-linked terrorists however, remained limited, and it seemed that Hamzah's links with extremist leaders were impeding the government's efforts to clamp down. By late May, Abu Bakar Bashir had still not been arrested, despite evidence from Singapore of his deep involvement in the Jemaah Islamiah plot there. Nevertheless, the TNI seemed to be exploiting Western interest in securing Indonesia's cooperation. The army benefited from greater leeway for using force to control internal security problems, particularly in Aceh. TNI commanders also apparently hoped that Jakarta's gestures on the terrorist issue would help soften Washington's position on military aid and arms sales. However, US Congressional legislation in late 2001 imposed new conditions on such links.[33] Congressional opposition even prevented Washington from funding counter-terrorist training for Polri.[34]

Displaced people and asylum-seekers

By late 2001, violence in East Timor, Papua, Aceh, Maluku, Sulawesi and Kalimantan had generated more than 1.3m displaced people within Indonesia, and exacerbated or created significant immigration-related problems for some regional states. As political tensions escalated in early 2001, the average daily number of Indonesians entering Malaysia illegally reached 3,000.[35] In February 2001, troops and police were deployed to prevent Indonesian refugees from crossing into Sabah and Sarawak.[36] Malaysia was already trying to use forced repatriation to reduce its population of almost one million illegal immigrants, most of whom are Indonesian. The illegal Indonesian presence has been held responsible for escalating crime and other social ills since the late 1990s.[37] The government has also been concerned over the strain imposed by illegal immigrants on the infrastructure (particularly water supplies), and the long-term threat they might pose to Malaysian sovereignty. Although 120,000 'illegals' were sent home during 2001, many quickly returned to Malaysia with assistance from Indonesian criminal syndicates and corrupt Malaysian officials.[38] In addition, there are almost 600,000 legal Indonesian workers in Malaysia. Violent incidents involving Indonesian workers in early 2002 reinforced the Malaysian government's long-standing determination to reduce the size of the Indonesian community.[39]

Indonesia's weakened law-enforcement apparatus has allowed asylum-seekers from third countries to use the country as a stepping-stone to Australia. Although the numbers involved have so far been relatively small, since the late 1990s the Australian government has claimed that it is facing an illegal-immigration crisis. The number of asylum-seekers reaching Australia grew from almost none in the early 1990s to approximately 4,000 – mainly from Afghanistan and Iraq – during 2001.[40] Virtually all these migrants travelled to Australia by way of Indonesia, their passage facilitated by the local branches of international criminal syndicates. Canberra has contained the number of asylum-seekers reaching Australia only by implementing extensive preventive measures, including holding asylum-seekers in spartan detention camps and paying South Pacific states to accommodate them while their status is assessed. Australia has also subsidised Indonesian holding centres for asylum-seekers, while helping Indonesia's police.[41] Australian assistance in maintaining the Indonesian navy's *Nomad* maritime-patrol aircraft, vital for detecting illicit shipping, has continued despite the overall reduction in military-to-military ties.

Although by 2001 the Indonesian authorities had prevented more than 1,600 people from departing for Australia, another 3,000 remained at large in the country. Jakarta also refused to accept responsibility for 400 refugees who landed on Christmas Island in the Indian Ocean in August 2001, and declined Australia's offer to build detention camps in Indonesia.[42] Jakarta initially denied responsibility when 350 asylum-seekers drowned after their Indonesian vessel sank en route to Christmas Island in October 2001, and only took action when embarrassing evidence emerged of police collusion with the criminal syndicate involved in the incident.[43] Following criticism by Australian Prime Minister Howard, in November 2001 the Indonesian authorities arrested several leading people-smugglers in Jakarta in connection with the incident.[44] Nevertheless, Indonesian naval chief Admiral Indroko Sastrowiryono claimed that allowing asylum-seekers' vessels to 'continue their journey' was a 'basic human right', and indicated that, far from obstructing them, his ships would assist their passage.[45]

The Indonesian government's general lack of capacity, including the absence of relevant legislation, preoccupation with other matters and concern not to shoulder a long-term refugee burden contributed to its failure to combat people-smuggling more effectively.[46] However, lingering resentment over Australia's intervention in East Timor probably also played a part. Canberra has nevertheless attempted to maintain and where possible improve collaboration. After the Christmas Island incident, Australia offered Indonesia funding to expand existing holding centres, as well as five new long-range police patrol boats.[47] In February 2002, the two countries jointly convened a regional conference in Bali on people-smuggling which accommodated Jakarta's wish that Indonesia alone should not be blamed for the problem.[48]

Australia's hard line against asylum-seekers was controversial, domestically as well as internationally, but against the background of 11 September it helped to secure the ruling conservative coalition's re-election in November 2001. The government had undoubtedly exaggerated the issue for domestic political purposes.[49] However, the evident near-paranoia over illegal immigration raised the question of how Australia's government and people might react to any future large-scale exodus of Indonesian 'boat people' – from Maluku or Irian Jaya, for instance – in the event of a more profound breakdown in Indonesia's domestic order.

In Singapore, the deterrent effect of strict policies against illegal immigration and the city-state's sophisticated border controls and coastal protection have combined to minimise illicit infiltration by Indonesians. However, Singapore has reason to worry how it would cope if Indonesians sought refuge there in large numbers. A specific concern relates to Indonesia's ethnic Chinese. In the past, Singapore has provided refuge for thousands of wealthy Indonesian Chinese and their money. Indonesia's total ethnic Chinese population probably exceeds seven million. An Indonesian crisis in which the Chinese were victimised might threaten Singapore with an influx sufficiently large not only to impose a serious infrastructural burden, but also to highlight to an unwelcome degree its status as an ethnic Chinese enclave in South-east Asia.

Although preoccupied with its own problems, Indonesia's other immediate neighbour, PNG, has been concerned over increased numbers of people seeking refuge from the conflict in Papua. While there are ethnic links across the border and considerable sympathy for the plight of Indonesia's Papuans, the PNG government has no wish to become embroiled in the conflict or to assume the burden of a refugee population. During the mid-1980s, more than 12,000 Indonesian Papuans crossed into PNG; most of them are still there. Subsequent influxes have been sporadic and smaller, but there is clear potential for large-scale population movements in the event of intensified conflict in Indonesian Papua.[50]

Threats to economic security

Indonesia's disarray threatens other states' economic security in several ways. Since the late 1990s Indonesia's instability and regional conflicts have escalated political risk in maritime South-east Asia, at just the time that China has emerged as a serious competitor for foreign investment. There is widespread appreciation in South-east Asia that Indonesia's economic recovery and political stabilisation are vital if the region as a whole is to prosper.

Another concern has focused on the physical security of investments and production facilities in Indonesia. In places, there have already been direct threats. In early 2001, the shutdown of

ExxonMobil's production in Aceh due to concerns over the plant's security forced customers in Japan and South Korea to seek alternative sources of natural-gas in Indonesia and further afield.[51] Despite the resumption of production in July 2001, the incident cast a shadow over the reliability of ExxonMobil's production in the face of continuing violence in Aceh.[52] There are also potential threats to the Freeport mining operation in Papua, and to Singapore's extensive investments in Riau.

Piracy, encouraged by economic hardship and the widespread breakdown in law and order, has emerged as a major concern since the late 1990s. In 1999, reported attacks on ships in Indonesian waters and the Malacca Strait almost doubled compared with 1998. During 2000, of a total of 469 reported attacks worldwide, 119 occurred in Indonesian waters, and 75 in the Malacca Strait (where none had been reported as recently as 1997, and only one in 1998).[53] Reported attacks on Singapore-owned ships more than doubled during 2000.[54] The increased vulnerability of vessels passing through the Malacca Strait, the world's busiest maritime corridor with 600 ship movements daily, has particularly concerned Japan, which derives 80% of its oil imports through this route. Insurance premiums for ships transiting Indonesian waters have increased substantially, and Japanese companies have considered alternative routes for oil tankers.[55] Pirates in the region are increasingly well-equipped, using faster boats equipped with radar, sophisticated communications and heavier weapons, and are demonstrably willing to use extreme violence. Some pirates are reportedly linked to GAM, while others may be former Indonesian navy personnel. There is also evidence that some belong to organised, transnational criminal syndicates.

It was clear by the late 1990s that closer regional cooperation was necessary to contain the problem. Operational collaboration against piracy largely remained limited to coordinated patrols by Indonesia, Malaysia and Singapore under bilateral agreements dating from 1992. While this collaboration essentially involves each state taking responsibility for patrolling its territorial waters, it does allow for the 'hot handover' of pursuit. Such coordination proved effective against an earlier upsurge in piracy, which was virtually eliminated by 1993, but seemed insufficient in the more adverse circumstances of the late 1990s. At the informal 'ASEAN+3' summit in November 1999, involving China, Japan and South Korea as well as the ASEAN governments, Japanese Prime Minister Keizo Obuchi pressed for greatly expanded anti-piracy cooperation. A subsequent meeting in Tokyo involving 15 interested Asian governments in May 2000 agreed a series of measures: mutual visits by patrol vessels, combined exercises, seminars on maritime law enforcement, experts' meetings and training for other states' personnel at Japanese coast guard establishments.[56]

Chinese objections to Japan's involvement in security matters beyond its own shores, as well as ASEAN's principle of non-interference, ruled out serious consideration of Obuchi's earlier proposal for joint anti-piracy patrols in South-east Asia involving Japanese coast guard vessels. Nevertheless, Japan has stepped up its security cooperation with states which share its interest in keeping the Malacca Strait open to shipping. Singapore's navy and Japan's Maritime Self-Defense Force have conducted 'goodwill exercises' in the Singapore Strait since 1996. In May 2000, Japan and Singapore decided to augment their annual defence-policy discussions, established in 1997, with military staff talks.[57] In November 2000, the Japanese coast guard held its first exercises with the Indian and Malaysian navies.[58] South Korea, like Japan economically dependent on energy supplies transiting the Malacca Strait, has pressed Indonesia to take action against piracy, and in March 2001 signed anti-piracy agreements with Singapore and Malaysia.[59]

Facing escalating international pressure for action, Jakarta eventually began to take the issue more seriously. In November 2000, Indonesia's navy announced that it would establish three new operational headquarters, at Batam in the Riau Islands, on Bangka and at Belawan, near Medan, to coordinate anti-piracy measures in the Malacca and Singapore straits.[60] Because of his evidently inadequate response to the problem, the commander of the navy's Western Fleet task force was replaced in March 2001.[61] In June 2001, the navy stormed and recaptured a hijacked ship off East Kalimantan.[62] Naval special forces were active against pirate hideouts 'in and around the Riau islands'.[63] However, the impact of funding cuts on Indonesia's navy and marine police, and the additional demands imposed by separatist and communal conflict, limited their capacity to deter and combat attacks on merchant shipping.[64] In addition, there was disagreement over whether responsibility for anti-piracy measures lay with the navy or the police. Nevertheless, during 2001 reported attacks in Indonesian waters declined to 91, and those in the Malacca Strait more dramatically to 17. According to the International Maritime Bureau's Piracy Reporting Centre in Kuala Lumpur, the reduction was due particularly to more aggressive patrolling by Malaysia's marine police.[65]

Indonesia and its surrounding seas remain the most dangerous part of the world for piracy, and concern within and outside the region remains acute. In September 2001, GAM warned that ships using the Malacca Strait should seek its 'permission' to ensure their security. Malaysia further intensified its marine police patrols in response.[66] As concerns grew over a potential terrorist threat to shipping, including supply vessels supporting US forces in Afghanistan, the US navy also despatched warships to patrol the Malacca Strait.[67] In April 2002, the Indian and US navies began the coordinated escorting of US merchant ships through the Strait.[68]

Environmental problems

The primary environmental threat Indonesia poses to its neighbours stems from forest fires. During 1997 and early 1998, fires in Sumatra, Kalimantan and other parts of Indonesia raged out of control, largely as a result of logging companies and plantation owners clearing land for palm-oil production. The result was the worst-ever atmospheric pollution (euphemistically referred to in the region as 'haze') over much of South-east Asia; states affected included Malaysia, Brunei and Singapore, as well as much of Indonesia. The pollution in Malaysia's state of Sarawak was so bad that a state of emergency was declared there in September 1997.[69] By 2001, the health-related costs of the 1997 fires were estimated at $8bn.[70]

The governments of those countries most seriously affected by the Indonesian fires protested in a low-key manner to Jakarta, and ASEAN devised a Regional Haze Action Plan. However, ASEAN's non-interference principle and the Suharto regime's reluctance to act against the business conglomerates responsible for most fires ensured that no significant action was taken.[71] Since May 1998, inadequate surveillance, weak law enforcement and the preoccupation of governments in Jakarta with other matters have allowed the problem to continue, despite tighter legislation.[72] There were significant new outbreaks of illegal burning in each subsequent year. In March 2002, Indonesian forestry officials claimed that they were 'powerless' to prevent fires; there were no plans to prosecute those responsible for recent outbreaks.[73]

Another major environmental-security concern is the potential for major oil spills from tankers, which would not only cause large-scale damage through pollution, but could also disrupt maritime traffic or even close the Malacca Strait.[74] The increase in maritime traffic resulting from East Asia's economic growth, together with the escalation in piracy (which could lead to tankers colliding or running aground), have accentuated concerns in Malaysia and Singapore.

The possibility of intervention

Despite the economic and political instruments at their disposal, the capacity of Indonesia's interlocutors in the West, Japan and South-east Asia to influence developments in the archipelago is limited. Beyond restrictions on military assistance and supplies, the application of sanctions to encourage reform has never been a serious option. However, the continued provision of political, economic and technical assistance – ranging from declarations of support for Indonesia's national integrity and IMF loans to more specific assistance with, for example, environmental management and the development of Polri – will help minimise the damaging security ramifications of Indonesia's protracted crisis. Military assistance from Western states is likely to remain limited until senior officers responsible for human-rights abuses have been brought to justice.

Indonesia's deteriorating domestic security environment has raised the possibility of military intervention there several times since the East Timor crisis. In June–July 2000, there was considerable agitation in Western Europe over the deteriorating situation in Maluku, where the beleaguered Christian community had called for international intervention; Abdurrahman claimed that UN Secretary-General Kofi Annan had told him that some Security Council members had pressed for the deployment of UN peacekeeping troops.[75] In September 2000, the killing of UN aid workers in the West Timorese border town of Atambua by pro-Indonesian militiamen sparked speculation that UN troops in East Timor might intervene across the border. In late 2000, the PDP in Papua called for UN military as well as diplomatic intervention in the province. And since late 2001, there have been suggestions in the international media that Indonesia's alleged links to international terrorism might precipitate some form of US or Western military involvement.

The likelihood of military intervention in each of these cases was minimal. Neither the Abdurrahman nor Megawati governments has been willing to accept a role for foreign forces in Indonesia's domestic affairs. And none of these cases was sufficiently critical to ensure a mandate from the UN Security Council like that which allowed the intervention in East Timor. Moreover, there was no strong inclination amongst Western governments, keen for a variety of reasons to maintain equable relations with Jakarta, for intervention in any of these contingencies. In relation to Indonesian terrorism, even the type of US military involvement seen in the Philippines since January 2002 is virtually unthinkable. In March 2002, US Deputy Secretary of Defense Wolfowitz argued that there was 'simply no need for that kind of thing in Indonesia'.[76]

Nevertheless, this does not preclude such intervention in the future. One conceivable scenario might be an escalation of conflict in Aceh, Papua, Maluku or elsewhere leading to large-scale human-rights abuses, perhaps on the scale seen in East Timor, and a humanitarian crisis. If the international media gave such a development a high profile, pressure would mount, particularly in the West, for the deployment of military observers or peacekeeping forces. Such international intervention would be most likely in the case of Papua, because of its proximity to Australia, its shared border with PNG and its largely Christian indigenous population. Negotiated, limited military intervention is also conceivable should deteriorating security threaten large numbers of foreign nationals, necessitating their rapid evacuation. In May 1998, Japan sent transport aircraft, military personnel and coast-guard ships to Singapore in readiness to evacuate Japanese nationals from Indonesia during the violent demonstrations against Suharto.

The most extreme, and unlikely, scenario would see Indonesia's degeneration into an 'Asian Yugoslavia'. The precise circumstances in which such a situation might occur are impossible to predict, but would probably involve some combination of protracted economic recession, weakened national leadership, rising religious extremism and growing tensions between the central government and increasingly confident regions, leading to a breakdown in Jakarta's authority and a series of complex emergencies throughout the archipelago. In the midst of widespread conflict between ethnic and religious communities, human-rights abuse would be widespread, generating large-scale movements of displaced people, not only within the archipelago, but also outwards towards neighbouring countries. The demands on neighbouring states to accommodate asylum-seekers could be huge. Indonesian secessionism could exacerbate existing centre–periphery tensions in Malaysia, the Philippines and Thailand.

The emergence of a number of weak mini-states could allow international criminal syndicates involved in people-smuggling and narcotics-trafficking, as well as militant groups with international terrorist connections, to establish bases. Fragmentation would also increase piracy, possibly fostered by warlords or renegade military commanders in breakaway provinces and districts, affecting sea lanes through the Malacca and other straits. This would have particularly important implications for those North-East Asian states (China and South Korea as well as Japan) that depend on Middle Eastern oil, but would also have wider ramifications for the international economy. At the same time, the US retains a vital interest in seeing that east–west routes through the archipelago (the Sunda, Lombok-Makassar, Ombai-Wetar as well as Malacca straits) remain open for the movement of naval forces and military logistics from its Pacific bases to the Indian Ocean and Middle East. Australia's key interest would be in maintaining north–south access through Indonesia for its trade with South-east Asia. The multiplication of power centres would complicate efforts to contain all these likely problems. Interested powers including some South-east Asian governments might attempt to develop special relationships with certain of the new states, with a view to securing economic and security interests. For example, Australia would take a close interest in Papua, and Singapore in the Riau Islands.

This cataclysmic scenario could lead interested regional and Western states to intervene militarily. There would undoubtedly be calls from embattled ethnic and religious groups within Indonesia for protection. Christian communities would be likely to appeal to the West and the UN. If seriously threatened, ethnic Chinese communities might appeal to Beijing for assistance. In the West, governments would come under pressure to defend such groups' human rights. Singapore, Malaysia and Australia would be interested in pre-empting large-scale population movements in their direction.

In the event of a widespread breakdown in order, there would be pressure on the UN Security Council to mandate observer and peacekeeping forces for various parts of the archipelago. The onus of any military intervention would fall in the first instance on regional states. Since the East Timor intervention in 1999, some states in Indonesia's neighbourhood, notably Australia and Singapore, have increased their defence spending. During 2000, there were discussions within ASEAN over a 'wider role' for members' armed forces in maintaining regional security. This apparently hinted at them playing a role in any future peacekeeping force in Indonesia's problem provinces, such as Aceh or Maluku.[77] Alternatively, ASEAN members might assist Indonesia's efforts to control its separatist problems. Indonesian Defence Minister Juwono Sudarsono spoke of other ASEAN states' armed forces being actively involved if there was a 'total breakdown of law and order'.[78] In addition, the US and European governments, and possibly Japan and South Korea, would probably deploy naval power to protect shipping lanes, although if Indonesia disintegrated, Washington might find itself under considerable pressure, particularly from Australia, to make a broader commitment.

The complications inherent in responding to such an extreme scenario explain why governments, in the region and beyond, have emphasised so strongly that they do not wish to see Indonesia disintegrate. Partly because of the lack of external support for secessionism, circumstances requiring substantial outside intervention remain unlikely. For the time being, the more pressing issue for other states is how to assist Indonesia to manage the security-related ramifications of its current disarray, while using economic and political instruments to encourage broader reform in the hope of pre-empting additional problems.

Conclusion

Tensions between the centre and the periphery, together with communal conflict, are likely to plague Indonesia for the foreseeable future. But it is by no means evident that these problems will lead to the country's demise as a political entity. Indonesia is, on balance, likely to survive, albeit possibly in a looser form. The extent to which the government pursues a broad reformist agenda will substantially influence the course of events. At the political level, two main types of reform will be essential: the remodelling of centre–periphery relations; and security-sector reform.

Overall, the devolution of power and resources under the decentralisation programme which began in January 2001 may be achieving its main objective of pre-empting secessionist tendencies in resource-rich regions such as East Kalimantan and Riau. There were many shortcomings in the original autonomy legislation, but it seems unlikely that any government in Jakarta could muster the will or capacity to reverse the process: Indonesia seems to be heading for a quasi-federal future. However, this experiment is fraught with dangers, not least that decentralisation has sometimes helped to precipitate communal violence by exacerbating local disputes over power and resources. Establishing a stable and mutually-acceptable pattern of relations between Jakarta, the provinces and sub-provincial units will probably take many years.

In Aceh and Papua, the special autonomy granted in January 2002 is unlikely to ease secessionist sentiment, which has resulted from decades of abuse and exploitation. The loss of these provinces is not inevitable, but for Jakarta to stand any chance of retaining them in the long term a much more profound process of reconciliation will be necessary. Justice for the victims of human-rights abuses dating back to the New Order would necessarily figure prominently in any peace settlement for either province. It would also be crucial to reduce substantially, or even end, the TNI's internal-security role in both provinces, as it is clear that the military has repeatedly stimulated rather than calmed the conflicts. A necessary quid pro quo would be the disarmament of the resistance movements.

Even to deal effectively with the problems of Aceh and Papua, much more profound security-sector reform is required than Megawati, or for that matter any likely presidential successor, presently envisages. Other key elements of reform would include the more thoroughgoing subjugation of the armed forces to civilian political authority, the rigorous enforcement of law on security-force personnel, the TNI's withdrawal from its socio-political function and territorial role, the ending of the military's commercial operations and the strengthening of the police force such that it can assume genuine primary responsibility for internal security.

Communal conflict has been much more widespread than armed separatism, and together with growing religious extremism may undermine national cohesion more seriously in the longer term. Because of the diverse factors that contribute to the breakdown of relations between ethnic or religious groups, such conflict is difficult to combat, particularly given continuing decentralisation. However, outside Java the strengthening of civil society, including the media and organisations that cut across communal lines such as labour unions and business associations, together with the development of a neutral and effective police force and judicial system, would go a long way towards forestalling further conflict. Throughout Indonesia, more effective local development strategies, including support for small and medium-sized enterprises, are needed to reduce the poverty that helps fuel radical Islamic movements.

While communal conflict and religious militancy do not directly threaten territorial disintegration, they do promise to weaken central-government control. Indonesia's economic and political frailty implies that the country will continue to generate a range of low-intensity and unconventional security concerns. Although their capacity to influence such a huge country's evolution is limited, other states do possess important instruments that could help to contain the security implications of Indonesia's protracted crisis. The most important is probably the willingness of industrialised states and multilateral financial institutions to help Indonesia manage its massive international debt, which haemorrhages national wealth that could otherwise be used for development purposes, including modernising the country's security sector and providing resources for the effective implementation of decentralisation.

Megawati's government will almost certainly survive until 2004, providing a degree of reassurance that Indonesia is unlikely to disintegrate in the short to medium term. But with the popularity of Megawati and the PDI-P apparently in decline, and Golkar and the Muslim parties facing disintegration, the nature of the next administration is difficult to predict. Nevertheless, certain potential presidential candidates might if they gained power deviate from the essentially reformist path followed by both Abdurrahman and Megawati, for instance by pursuing more populist economic policies, supporting the insertion of the Jakarta Charter into the constitution, or accommodating TNI interests to a greater extent. The consequences for Indonesia's national cohesion could be catastrophic. While a complete breakdown in Jakarta's authority remains unlikely, concerned neighbours and interested powers will need to coordinate their planning for such a contingency.

Notes

Acknowledgements

The author thanks Sally Harris for her research assistance.

Chapter 1

1 Harold Crouch, 'Indonesia: Democratization and the Threat of Disintegration', *Southeast Asian Affairs 2000* (Singapore: Institute of Southeast Asian Studies, 2000), pp. 119–20.
2 Arief Budiman, 'Indonesia: The Trials of President Wahid', *ibid.*, pp. 150–52.
3 'TNI in Business: Money Needed', *Straits Times*, 15 June 2000.
4 Nayan Chanda, John McBeth and Dan Murphy, 'Wahid's Coming Clash', *Far Eastern Economic Review*, 3 February 2000, pp. 8–11.
5 'Indonesian General Defies President's Call To Resign', *Straits Times*, 3 February 2000.
6 'Coup Could Cause Riots', *ibid.*, 19 January 2000.
7 Susan Sim, 'Backing for Gus Dur as Wiranto Exits Cabinet', *ibid.*, 15 February 2000.
8 'Gus Dur's Coup on His Top Generals', *ibid.*, 1 March 2000.
9 'Widodo Says Military Ready To Quit Parliament', *ibid.*, 26 February 2000; 'TNI's Business Empire Faces Audit', *ibid.*, 2 March 2000; 'Gus Dur Scraps Security Agency', *ibid.*, 9 March 2000; 'Press On With Reforms, Juwono Says', *ibid.*, 13 March 2000.
10 'Minister on Preserving Independence of Defence Department', *Suara Karya*, 26 April 2000, in SWB/FE/3825 B/4, 27 April 2000.
11 'TNI in Business'.
12 A. Hasnan Habib, 'The Future of the Indonesian Armed Forces', draft paper, March 2000.
13 'Military To Withdraw Local Officers in "Reformist Step"', *Kompas*, 27 April 2000, in SWB/FE/3826 B/2, 28 April 2000.
14 'Press On With Reforms'.
15 Irman G. Lanti, 'Lessons from Gus Dur's Failed Presidency', *Straits Times*, 1 August 2001.
16 'Army Chief: Security Comes Before Politics and Economy', *Jakarta Post*, 9 January 2001.

[17] 'Banser Prepare for Mass-mobilization', *ibid.*, 11 January 2001; 'Demonstrations by Gus Dur Supporters Turn Violent', *ibid.*, 6 February 2001.

[18] Sadanand Dhume and Dini Djalal, 'Wahid's Fight against Hope', *Far Eastern Economic Review*, 14 June 2001, pp. 32–33.

[19] Seth Mydans, 'Indonesians Warned by Wahid of Emergency', *International Herald Tribune*, 10 July 2001; 'Wahid Acts To Suspend Parliament', *ibid.*, 23 July 2001.

[20] Peter Carey, 'Defying Gravity', *World Today*, vol. 57, no. 8–9, August–September 2001, p. 16.

[21] 'Indonesians "Misused $2b in State Funds"', *Straits Times*, 27 September 2001.

[22] Mark Landler, 'Jakarta's Markets Warm to Megawati', *International Herald Tribune*, 25 July 2001; 'Indonesia Set for Revival of Cronyism', *Straits Times*, 7 August 2001.

[23] 'Indonesia: Wahid Ouster Not Mega Triumph?', *Asia Monitor South East Asia*, vol. 12, no. 9, September 2001, p. 5.

[24] 'Police on Alert after Fuel Price Increase', *Straits Times*, 18 June 2001.

[25] J. Soedjati Djiwandono, 'Megawati's Cabinet, the Best Since Soeharto?', *Jakarta Post*, 10 August 2001.

[26] Sidhesh Kaul, 'Dynasties, Spouses: Lesson for Megawati', *ibid.*, 22 August 2001.

[27] Michael Richardson, 'Military Regains Political Clout', *International Herald Tribune*, 24 July 2001.

[28] Seth Mydans, 'Megawati Plots a Course', *ibid.*, 17 August 2001.

[29] 'Megawati Names Rainbow Cabinet', *Jakarta Post*, 10 August 2001.

[30] 'A Message from Mega', *ibid.*, 11 August 2001; 'Ministers Warned of Nepotism', *ibid.*, 16 August 2001.

[31] 'MPR Fails To Agree on Constitutional Reforms', *ibid.*, 10 November 2001.

[32] Derwin Pereira, 'Mega Paints Vision of a "New Indonesia"', *Straits Times*, 17 August 2001.

[33] 'Megawati Signals Readiness To Prosecute Militias', *ibid.*, 7 August 2001; Pereira, 'Mega Paints Vision'.

[34] Tom McCawley, 'Indonesia Reaches IMF Accord over Stalled Loan', *Financial Times*, 28 August 2001.

[35] 'Crackdown on Anti-US Protests', *Asia Monitor South East Asia*, vol. 12, no. 11, November 2001, p. 5; Robert Go, '$5.7b in Loans for Indonesia', *Straits Times*, 9 November 2001.

[36] Kornelius Purba, 'Megawati Must Assume More Control', *Jakarta Post*, 31 October 2001.

[37] 'Crisis and Firm Leadership', *ibid.*, 10 October 2001; Susanto Pudjomartono, 'Megawati Must Change Her Leadership Management', *ibid.*, 22 October 2001; Dadan Wijaksana, 'Mega Seen as Moving Too Slowly in Resolving Economic Woes', *ibid.*, 30 October 2001.

[38] 'Foreign Investment in Indonesia Fell Nearly 42% in 2001', *Straits Times*, 19 January 2002.

[39] Davi Asmarani, 'Jakarta "Has Failed To Lift the Economy"', *ibid.*, 11 January 2002; 'Indonesia's GDP Growth Halves to 1.6%', *ibid.*, 19 February 2002.

[40] 'Intrusive Legislature', *Jakarta Post*, 4 October 2001.

[41] Sadanand Dhume, 'High Noon in Provincial Padang', *Far*

Eastern Economic Review, 15 November 2001, pp. 16–19.

[42] Sarwono Kusumaadmadja, quoted in John McBeth, 'Nothing Changes', *ibid.*, 1 November 2001, p. 18.

[43] Kurniawan Hari, 'Megawati Fails To Live Up to Reform Hopes: Experts', *Jakarta Post*, 31 October 2001.

[44] Devi Asmarani, 'Witnesses Against Tommy Recant', *Straits Times*, 10 April 2002.

[45] John McBeth and Dini Djalal, 'The Benefits of Prosecution', *Far Eastern Economic Review*, 28 March 2002, pp. 12–16.

[46] Bambang Nurbianto, 'Military Rebuilding Political Power Base, Observers Warn', *Jakarta Post*, 8 January 2002; Devi Asmarani, 'Trial Will Test Mega's Ties with Military', *Straits Times*, 3 January 2002; Marianne Kearney, 'Five Graft Cases in Recent Days: Jakarta Shows It Means Business', *ibid.*, 20 March 2002.

[47] Imanuddin, 'Why the Delay in Search for New TNI Chief?', *Jakarta Post*, 7 January 2002; John McBeth and Michael Vatikiotis, 'An About-Turn on the Military', *Far Eastern Economic Review*, 25 April 2002, pp. 12–15.

[48] Fabiola Desy Unidjaja, 'Megawati Paints Grim Economic Picture', *Jakarta Post*, 2 November 2001.

[49] Robert Go, 'Indonesians Surprised by Fuel-price Hike', *Straits Times*, 18 January 2002.

[50] Devi Asmarani, 'Golkar Torn Apart', *ibid.*, 30 January 2002.

Chapter 2

[1] See, for example, 'Disintegration Dreaded', *The Economist*, 9 December 2000, p. 86.

[2] 'Army Chief Says Threat of National Disintegration "Extremely Serious"', Televisi Republik Indonesia, Jakarta, 26 January 2000, in SWB/FE 3749 B/3, 28 January 2000.

[3] Derwin Pereira, 'Aceh, Irian Jaya May Secede, Amien Warns', *Straits Times*, 18 October 2000.

[4] 'Indonesia in Danger of Collapsing: Lemhannas', *Jakarta Post*, 26 November 2000.

[5] Robert Cribb, *Historical Atlas of Indonesia* (Richmond: Curzon Press, 2000), p. 162.

[6] M. C. Ricklefs, *A History of Modern Indonesia* (Basingstoke: Palgrave, 2001), pp. 308–10.

[7] See Audrey R. Kahin and George McT. Kahin, *Subversion as Foreign Policy: The Secret Eisenhower and Dulles Debacle in Indonesia* (New York: The New Press, 1995).

[8] Anne Booth, 'Indonesia: Will Decentralisation Lead to Disintegration?', paper presented at the EUROSEAS conference, London, 6–8 September 2001, p. 8.

[9] *Ibid.*

[10] *Ibid.*, pp. 9–12.

[11] *Ibid.*, pp. 22–25.

[12] *Ibid.*, p. 23.

[13] *Ibid.*, p. 18.

[14] 'On Threshold of Independence', *Jakarta Post*, 7 September 2001.

[15] Tim Kell, *The Roots of Acehnese Rebellion* (Ithaca, NY: Cornell Modern Indonesia Project, 1995), pp. 8–10.

[16] *Ibid.*, pp. 13–19.

[17] Ricklefs, *A History of Modern Indonesia*, p. 388.

[18] Kell, *The Roots of Acehnese Rebellion*, pp. 74–75.

[19] Samantha F. Ravich, 'Eyeing Indonesia Through the Lens of Aceh', *Washington Quarterly*, vol. 23, no. 3, Summer 2000, p. 14.

[20] Rizal Sukma, 'The Acehnese Rebellion: Secessionist Movement in Post-Suharto Indonesia', in Andrew T. H. Tan and J. D. Kenneth Boutin (eds), *Non-Traditional Security Issues in South-east Asia* (Singapore: Select Publishing, 2001), p. 390.

[21] International Crisis Group, *Aceh: Escalating Tension*, Indonesia Briefing (Banda Aceh/Jakarta/Brussels: International Crisis Group, December 2000), p. 4.

[22] Irwan Firdaus, 'Independence Rally Draws a Million in Aceh Province', *The Guardian*, 9 November 1999.

[23] Diarmid O'Sullivan, 'Wahid Agrees to Ballot on Aceh's Independence', *Financial Times*, 5 November 1999; 'Indonesia's Leader Rejects Call for Martial Law in Aceh', *International Herald Tribune*, 25 November 1999.

[24] *Jawa Pos* website, 7 December 1999, in SWB/FE 3713 B/4, 9 December 1999.

[25] *Aceh: Escalating Tension*, p. 5.

[26] 'Now Aceh Takes a Beating', *The Economist*, 11 March 2000, p. 87.

[27] 'At Least 1,041 Killed in Aceh in One Year', *Jakarta Post*, 28 January 2001.

[28] Rajiv Chandrasekaran, 'Aceh Aid Worker Reports Execution-style Killings', *International Herald Tribune*, 14 December 2000.

[29] *Aceh: Escalating Tension*, p. 4.

[30] 'Civil Emergency Status the Last Resort: Widodo', *Jakarta Post*, 25 November 2000.

[31] 'Expectations High for New Accord in Aceh', *Ibid.*, 18 February 2001; 'Ceasefire in Aceh Extended Indefinitely', *Straits Times*, 18 February 2001.

[32] 'Other Firms in Aceh Close after Exxon Shutdown', *ibid.*, 12 March 2001.

[33] International Crisis Group, *Aceh: Why Military Force Won't Bring Lasting Peace*, ICG Asia Report 17 (Jakarta/Brussels: International Crisis Group, June 2001), p. 8.

[34] 'TNI To Proceed with Deployment of Troops in Aceh', *Jakarta Post*, 21 April 2001.

[35] Marianne Kearney, 'Bloodshed in Aceh Not Bending People', *Straits Times*, 24 May 2001.

[36] '27 Bodies Found in Aceh Amid Peace Talks', *ibid.*, 3 July 2001; 'Indonesian Police Arrest Negotiators', *New Straits Times*, 21 July 2001.

[37] Derwin Pereira, 'Mega Offers Aceh More Autonomy', *Straits Times*, 16 August 2001.

[38] International Crisis Group, *Aceh: Can Autonomy Stem the Conflict?*, ICG Asia Report 18 (Jakarta/Brussels: International Crisis Group, June 2001), p. 14.

[39] 'Folly of Military Option', *Jakarta Post*, 29 August 2001.

[40] Derwin Pereira, 'Elite Troops Hunt Aceh Rebel Chief', *Straits Times*, 31 October 2001.

[41] 'Aceh Killings a Wake-Up Call', *Jakarta Post*, 29 August 2001.

[42] Fabiola Desy Unidjaja, 'Government Vows To Be Tougher in Restive Areas', *ibid.*, 30 November 2001.

[43] 'Six Killed in Aceh as Separatists Mark Struggle, *Straits Times*, 5 December 2001.

[44] Fabiola Desy Unidjaja, 'Military Command Reinstated in Aceh', *Jakarta Post*, 11 January 2002.

[45] Ibnu Mat Noor, 'Military Kills GAM Chief in Gun Battle', *ibid.*, 24 January 2002.

[46] 'Aceh: 12 Hurt in Grenade Blast Outside Shopping Mall', *Straits Times*, 12 February 2002.

[47] *Aceh: Can Autonomy Stem the Conflict?*, pp. 19–21.

[48] *Ibid.*, p. 12.

[49] Mieke Kooistra, *Indonesia: Regional Conflicts and State Terror* (London: Minority Rights Group International, 2001), p. 23.

[50] 'Irian Jaya Leaders Declare Independence', *Straits Times*, 5 June 2000.

[51] 'Papuan Flag Allowed To Fly Again in Irian Jaya', *Kompas*, 14 June 2000, in SWB/FE 3868 B/3, 16 June 2000.

[52] 'Clashes in Irian Jaya Over Separatist Flags', *Straits Times*, 7 October 2000.

[53] Richard Chauvel, 'Jakarta's Strategy To Deal with Papuan Nationalism', *Jakarta Post*, 28 November 2001.

[54] 'Irian Jaya Spokesman Says Indonesian Army "Nurturing Undercover Support"', *Radio Australia*, 29 November 2000, in SWB/FE/ 4012 B/3, 1 December 2000.

[55] 'Irian Jaya Pro-Independence Council Seeks UN Intervention in Province', *ibid.*, 14 December 2000, in SWB/FE/4024 B/2, 15 December 2000.

[56] 'Papuan Proposal Seeks Wide-Ranging Autonomy', *Jakarta Post*, 21 April 2001.

[57] 'Irian Jaya Forum Delegates Reject Autonomy, Demand Independence', *Kompas*, 29 November 2001, in SWB/ FE/4108 B/3, 30 March 2001.

[58] 'West Papuan Pro-Independence Leaders Split Over Benefits of Autonomy', *Radio Australia*, 27 September 2000, in SWB/FE/ 3958 B/3, 29 September 2000.

[59] 'Papua Bill Endorsed in Flurry Before Recess', *Jakarta Post*, 23 October 2001.

[60] Neles Kebadabi Tebay, 'Why Autonomy Is Not Well Received by Papuans', *ibid.*, 15 December 2001.

[61] Bob Lowry, 'Irian Jaya: Can the Time Bomb Be Defused?', *Asia-Pacific Defence Reporter*, February 2001, pp. 78–79.

[62] Marianne Kearney, 'Jakarta Feels Heat Over Theys' Death', *Straits Times*, 14 November 2001.

[63] *Aceh: Why Military Force Won't Bring Lasting Peace*, p. 12.

[64] *Ibid.*, p. iii; Tiarma Siboro, 'Conflicts Worsen Despite Troop Deployments', *Jakarta Post*, 3 December 2001.

[65] *Aceh: Escalating Tension*, pp. 2, 4.

[66] Lesley McCulloch, *Trifungsi: The Role of the Indonesian Military in Business*, Bonn International Centre for Conversion, www.bicc.de/budget/events/ milbus/confpapers.html

[67] *Aceh: Why Military Force Won't Bring Lasting Peace*, p. 14.

[68] *Aceh: Escalating Tension*, p. 3.

[69] 'West Papua Independence Movement Infiltrated by Indonesian Agents', *Radio New Zealand International*, 5 December 2000, in SWB/FE/ 4016 B/5, 6 December 2000; Marianne Kearney, 'Irian Jaya: Will It Be Another Timor?', *Straits Times*, 14 December 2000.

[70] 'Locals Ignore "Free Riau Forces" Warning on Flag Raising', *RiauGlobal* website, 20 August 2000, in SWB/FE/ 3925 B/2, 22 August 2000.

[71] 'If I Go, So Does Indonesia', *Straits Times*, 24 March 2001.

[72] 'Shoot First, Ask Questions Later', *Laksamana.net*, 5 January 2002, http://laksamana.net/ vnews.cfm?ncat=35&news_id=1766

[73] Booth, 'Indonesia', pp. 2–3.

[74] 'VP Criticizes Regional Autonomy Law', *Jakarta Post*, 17 May 2001; Joe Leahy and Taufan Hidayat, 'Megawati Plan for Provinces', *Financial Times*, 31 July 2001.

75 'Indonesia Risks Becoming Like Balkans: Mega', *Straits Times*, 29 October 2001; Fabiola Desy Unidjaja, 'Unity in Danger, Mega Warns', *Jakarta Post*, 30 October 2001.

76 'Autonomy Law Reviewed To Save Unitary State', *ibid.*, 4 September 2001.

77 Sadanand Dhume, 'A Windfall for Riau', *Far Eastern Economic Review*, 21 February 2002, p. 43.

78 Annastashya Emmanuelle, 'Megawati Still Pushing for Autonomy Revision', *Jakarta Post*, 29 January 2002.

79 Margot Cohen, 'Autonomy Rules, OK?', *Far Eastern Economic Review*, 2 August 2001, pp. 55–58.

80 *Aceh: Can Autonomy Stem the Conflict?*, pp. 5, 8.

81 *Ibid.*, p. 16.

82 Bambang Nurbianto, 'Now Bill Tightens Rules on Election Contestants', *Jakarta Post*, 16 November 2001.

83 'Nationalism Remains Strong: CESDA Survey', *ibid.*, 15 August 2001.

84 '10 Regions Submit Proposals Demanding Provincial Status', *Ibid.*, 14 February 2001.

85 'President on Autonomous, Federalist Future', *Famiglia Cristiana* (Milan), 20 February 2000, in SWB/FE/3769 B/4, 21 February 2000.

Chapter 3

1 'Maluku Conflict Has Claimed About 9,000 Lives', *Jakarta Post*, 6 September 2001.

2 'Holy War in the Spice Islands', *The Economist*, 17 March 2001.

3 'No Tolerance of Separatism in Maluku: Pattimura Military Chief', *Jakarta Post*, 26 August 2001.

4 Gerry van Klinken, 'The Maluku Wars: Bringing Society Back In', *Indonesia*, 71, April 2001, p. 12.

5 *Ibid.*, pp. 10–12.

6 *Ibid.*, pp. 20–23.

7 'Maluku Dialog Ends with Peace Commitment', *Jakarta Post*, 22 March 2001.

8 'Christian, Muslim Leaders Reach Maluku Peace Pact', *Straits Times*, 14 February 2002.

9 Robert Go, 'Ambon on Alert after Arrest of Radical Leader', *ibid.*, 6 May 2002.

10 John McBeth, 'Beyond the Pale', *Far Eastern Economic Review*, 20 January 2000, p. 17.

11 Smith Alhader, 'The Forgotten War in North Maluku', *Inside Indonesia*, 63, July–September 2000, http://www.insideindonesia.org/edit63/alhader.htm

12 Marianne Kearney, 'Over 100 Killed in New Maluku Violence', *Straits Times*, 21 June 2000; van Klinken, 'The Maluku Wars', pp. 5–7.

13 Kearney, 'Over 100 Killed'; John Aglionby, 'Rescued Confirm Ferry Sank Killing Hundreds', *The Guardian*, 3 July 2000.

14 'Troops in Maluku To Be Gradually Pulled Out', *Jakarta Post*, 19 January 2001.

15 'North Maluku Refugees Repatriated', *ibid.*, 27 February 2001; 'Muslims, Christians Make Peace', *ibid.*, 23 May 2001.

16 Van Klinken, 'The Maluku Wars', p. 10.

17 'Indonesia Army Accused of Massacre', *The Times*, 13 August 1999; 'Sunday Killings a Setback for Gus Dur', *Straits Times*, 26 January 2000; 'Indonesia To Withdraw "Rogue" Moluccas Forces', *International Herald*

Tribune, 28 June 2000; John Aglionby, 'TV Film Shows Army Bias in Moluccas Fighting', *The Guardian*, 18 July 2000.

18 'Police Fight Marines in Ambon, One Dead', *Astaga* website, 17 October 2000, in SWB/FE/ 3974 B/2, 18 October 2000; 'Police, Military Chiefs Meet To Clear the Air', *Jakarta Post*, 7 February 2001.

19 Tiarma Siboro, 'Security Forces an Obstacle to Peace in Maluku: Mayor', *ibid.*, 23 January 2002.

20 Irfan S. Awwas, 'Withdraw Joint Troops from Ambon', *ibid.*, 29 January 2001.

21 Seth Mydans, 'Indonesian Conflict May Be Breeding the Terrorists of Tomorrow', *International Herald Tribune*, 11 January 2002.

22 David Rohde, 'Indonesia Unraveling?', *Foreign Affairs*, vol. 80, no. 4, July–August 2001, pp. 119–22.

23 *Ibid.*

24 'The Black Bats Strike Back', *The Economist*, 11 August 2001, p. 34.

25 Marianne Kearney, 'Sulawesi Bloodletting a Result of Weak Leadership', *Straits Times*, 8 December 2001.

26 'Central Sulawesi: Soldiers Questioned in Clashes', *ibid.*, 22 June 2000; John McBeth and Oren Murphy, 'Bloodbath', *Far Eastern Economic Review*, 6 July 2000, p. 22.

27 Santi W. E. Soekanto, 'Profiting from Violence in Eastern Indonesia', *Jakarta Post*, 3 December 2001.

28 Derwin Pereira, 'Sulawesi Strife Highlights Acute Police–Army Rivalry', *Straits Times*, 16 December 2001.

29 Marianne Kearney, 'Jakarta To Send 2,600 More Troops to Violence-Hit Sulawesi', *ibid.*, 4 December 2001.

30 'Factions in Sulawesi Agree To End Conflict', *ibid.*, 21 December 2001.

31 Human Rights Watch, *Communal Violence in West Kalimantan*, http://www.hrw.og/reports/ 1997/wkali

32 Marianne Kearney, 'Pontianak Clash Could Spin Out Of Control', *Straits Times*, 28 October 2000; 'Violence Continues in West Kalimantan Capital', *Jakarta Post*, 26 June 2001.

33 'Police Confirm the Arrest of Provocateurs', *ibid.*, 5 May 2001.

34 'No More Madurese, Say Dayaks', *Deutsche Presse-Agentur*, 7 March 2001, *BruNet* homepage, http://www.brunet.bn/news/ bb/wed/world/mar7w1.htm; 'C. Kalimantan Violence Claims Five More Lives', *Jakarta Post*, 2 April 2001.

35 Derwin Pereira, 'Armed Forces "Misread" Kalimantan Clashes', *Straits Times*, 5 March 2001.

36 Rajiv Chandrasekaran, 'Borneo Security Forces Clash with Each Other', *International Herald Tribune*, 28 February 2001.

37 'Government Issues 4-Point Initiative for Ethnic Conflict', *Televisi Republik Indonesia*, 8 March 2001, in SWB/FE/4091 B/2, 10 March 2001.

38 George J. Aditjondro, 'Avoiding the Mistakes of Ambon', *Jakarta Post*, 1 March 2001.

39 Rohde, 'Indonesia Unraveling?', p. 122; 'Madurese and Dayak Sign Peace Deal', *ibid.*, 30 March 2001; 'North Sulawesi Ready To Ward Off Violence', *Jakarta Post*, 31 March 2001.

40 Devi Asmarani, 'Islamic Parties Keep Up the Pressure To

Include Shariah Law', *Straits Times*, 6 November 2001; Marianne Kearney, 'Muslims Want Secular Indonesia', *ibid.*, 15 February 2002.

41 'Proposed Jakarta Charter Sparks Demonstrations in West Timor, Capital', *Bali Post* website, 16 August 2000, in SWB/FE/3921 B/3, 17 August 2000.

42 'North Sulawesi Threatens To Secede Over Jakarta Charter', *Manado Post* website, 7 August 2000, in SWB/FE/3915 B/4, 10 August 2000.

43 'Religious Freedom Comes Under Fire', *Far Eastern Economic Review*, 16 May 2002, p. 8.

44 Azyumardi Azra, 'Challenge of Political Islam to Megawati', *Jakarta Post*, 21 November 2001.

45 Tom McCawley, 'Islamic Groups Target Eastern Indonesia', *Financial Times*, 12 February 2002.

46 Derwin Pereira, 'Islamic Power Play', *Straits Times*, 19 November 2000.

47 Dini Djalal, 'Missed Opportunities', *Far Eastern Economic Review*, 31 January 2002, p. 22.

48 Pereira, 'Islamic Power Play'.

49 Derwin Pereira, 'Jakarta Action against Militants Impeded by V-P', *Straits Times*, 16 May 2002.

50 'PPP Admits Lack of Support for Reinstatement of Jakarta Charter', *Jakarta Post*, 5 September 2001.

Chapter 4

1 'President Abdurrahman Lashes Out at Singapore', *Jakarta Post*, 26 November 2000.

2 'Indonesia Proposes ASEAN Set Up New Group To Focus on East of Region', Kyodo news service, 25 November 2000, in SWB/FE/4008 S1/1, 27 November 2000.

3 'Howard, Gus Dur Pledge New Era', *Straits Times*, 27 June 2001.

4 'Emphasis on Bilateral Ties Back on Foreign Policy Agenda', *Jakarta Post*, 22 August 2001.

5 'Indonesia Should Become ASEAN's "Big Brother" in the Real Sense: Megawati', *ibid.*, 26 August 2001.

6 'Asean Has To Regain Lost Ground Fast', *Straits Times*, 29 September 2001.

7 Daojiong Zha, 'China and the May 1998 Riots of Indonesia: Exploring the Issues', *Pacific Review*, vol. 13, no. 4, 2000, pp. 557–75.

8 Konrad Muller, 'Manila and Muslim Insurgents Have a Lot of Talking To Do', *International Herald Tribune*, 9 May 2000; 'Foreign Secretary Warns of Regional Impact of Indonesian Separatism', *Radio Australia*, 18 November 1999, in SWB/FE/3696 B/6, 19 November 1999.

9 'ASEAN Leaders Rally Round PM's Proposal', *Singapore Bulletin*, vol. 27, no. 12, December 1999, p. 4; 'Asean Backs Indonesia Against Provinces', *Straits Times*, 26 July 2000.

10 'Instability in Indonesia Worries KL: Analysts', *ibid.*, 14 February 2000.

11 'Wahid Urges ASEAN Non-Interference over Malaysia's Anwar', *Radio Australia*, 27 November 2000, in SWB/FE/4010 B/2, 29 November 2000; 'Opposition "Seeking Indonesian Help"', *Straits Times*, 15 April 2001; 'Malaysia Asks RI Not To Support "Reformasi" Movement', *Jakarta Post*, 17 April 2001.

12 'Government To Prevent Entry of Indonesian Refugees from

Central Kalimantan', *Utusan Malaysia* website, 26 February 2001, in SWB/FE/4081 B/5, 27 February 2001.

[13] Brendan Pereira, 'Police: Militants in Cross-Border Crimes', *Straits Times,* 18 August 2001.

[14] 'RP Ship Captured for Carrying Guns', *Jakarta Post,* 16 January 2001; Sa-nguan Khumrungroj, 'Bid To Block Arms Route', *The Nation* (Bangkok), 15 May 2001; 'No Arms Smuggling in Strait of Malacca: Chief', *Jakarta Post,* 28 August 2001.

[15] Leslie Lau, 'KL Uncovers Plan To Set Up Union of Islamic States', *Straits Times,* 2 September 2001.

[16] Don Greenlees, 'Bin Laden Moves In On Indonesia', *The Australian,* 4 September 2001.

[17] Fabiola Desy Unidjaja, 'US Showers Indonesia with Promises', *Jakarta Post,* 21 September 2001.

[18] Rajiv Chandrasekaran, 'Indonesian Radicals Raise Threat to Westerners', *International Herald Tribune,* 9 October 2001.

[19] 'Jakarta Urges US Care in Retaliation', *Financial Times,* 1 October 2001.

[20] Fabiola Desy Unidjaja and Tiarma Siboro, 'Hamzah Demands US Stop Attack on Afghans', *Jakarta Post,* 14 October 2001.

[21] 'Terrorists? Jakarta "Yet To See Proof"', *Straits Times,* 22 January 2002.

[22] 'Of Missiles and Terrorism', *Far Eastern Economic Review,* 8 November 2001, p. 23.

[23] Dominic Nathan, '15 Nabbed Here for Terror Plans', *Straits Times,* 6 January 2002.

[24] Luz Baguioro, 'Militant Bomb-Maker Caught', *ibid.,* 19 January 2002.

[25] Brendan Pereira, 'All Signs of Miltancy Point to Link with Jakarta', *ibid.,* 24 January 2002.

[26] 'Officials Can't Agree on Al-Qaeda Presence in Sulawesi', *ibid.,* 15 December 2001.

[27] Derwin Pereira, 'Militants in Region "Plan To Strike Back"', *ibid.,* 11 February 2002.

[28] Murray Hiebert and Susan V. Lawrence, 'Hands Across the Ocean', *Far Eastern Economic Review,* 14 March 2002, p. 21.

[29] 'Bill Could Up the Pressure on Jakarta', *Ibid.,* 21 February 2002, p. 11.

[30] Derwin Pereira, 'Cleric Praises "Brave Osama"', *Straits Times,* 25 January 2002.

[31] Derwin Pereira, 'After S'pore Talks, Jakarta Sets Up Anti-Terror Force', *ibid.,* 9 February 2002.

[32] 'Indonesia "Needs Laws To Fight Terror"', *ibid.,* 31 January 2002.

[33] 'Mixed Blessings for Indonesia', *Far Eastern Economic Review,* 8 November 2001, p. 10; Sadanand Dhume and Murray Hiebert, 'A Slow March', *ibid.,* 17 January 2002, p. 26.

[34] 'US Offers $18m To Stiffen Jakarta's Anti-Terrorism Efforts', *Straits Times,* 29 January 2002; Lee Kim Chew, 'America in Policy Bind over Indonesia', *ibid.,* 20 May 2002.

[35] Leslie Lau, 'KL Worried over Turmoil in Jakarta', *ibid.,* 3 February 2001.

[36] 'Government To Prevent Entry of Indonesian Refugees from Central Kalimantan', *Utusan Malaysia* website, 26 February 2001, in SWB/FE/4081 B/4, 27 February 2001.

[37] 'Indonesian Migrants Top KL List of Most-Wanted', *Straits Times,* 2 July 2001.

[38] 'Graft and Lax Law Enforcement To Blame for Illegals', *ibid.*, 8 February 2002; '"Futile" To Deport Illegals to Sumatra', *ibid.*, 10 February 2002; Lesley Lau, 'Amnesty Offer for One Million Illegals', *ibid.*, 21 March 2002.

[39] 'KL Fears the 900,000 Workers Are Getting Out Of Control', *ibid.*, 28 January 2002.

[40] Shawn Donnan, 'Tide of Boat People Stirs Australia's Siege Mentality', *Financial Times*, 19 November 1999.

[41] Roger Maynard, 'Australia Finds "Home" for Illegals in Australia', *Straits Times*, 24 August 2001; John McBeth, 'To Turn a Tide', *Far Eastern Economic Review*, 13 September 2001, p. 20.

[42] 'Govt Sees Increase in Illegal Immigrants a Serious Problem', *Jakarta Post*, 19 September 2001.

[43] Marianne Kearney, 'Jakarta Nabs Cops over People Smuggling', *Straits Times*, 27 October 2001.

[44] Ian Timberlake, 'People Smugglers Disappear Amid Crackdown', *ibid.*, 17 November 2001.

[45] 'Australia's Hard Stance on Illegals "Paying Off"', *ibid.*, 1 November 2001.

[46] '"RI Cannot Deter" the Influx of Illegal Migrants', *Jakarta Post*, 4 September 2001.

[47] 'Australia To Fund Refugee Centres', *Financial Times*, 8–9 September 2001; Ian Bostock, 'Australia May Fund Indonesian Patrol Boats', *Jane's Defence Weekly*, 12 December 2001, p. 15.

[48] Co-chairs' statement, Bali Ministerial Conference on People-Smuggling, Trafficking in Persons and Related Transnational Crime, Bali, 26–28 February 2002, Commonwealth of Australia Department of Foreign Affairs and Trade website, http://www.dfat.gov.au/illegal_immigration/cochair.html

[49] Virginia Marsh, 'Canberra in Hot Water over Refugee "Crisis"', *Financial Times*, 12 December 2001.

[50] 'Country Report: Papua New Guinea', Worldwide Refugee Information, US Committee for Refugees website, http://www.refugees.org/world/countryrpt/easia_pacific/papua_new_guinea.htm

[51] 'Indonesian Army Moves To Retake Gas Field', *Financial Times*, 16 March 2001.

[52] 'ExxonMobil Resumes Production at Indonesia's Arun Plant', *LNG in World Markets*, vol. 13, no. 7, June 2001, pp. 8–9.

[53] 'Piracy in South-east Asia: Obstacles to Security Cooperation', *Strategic Comments*, IISS, vol. 6, no. 5, June 2000; Russell Barling, 'Pirates Find Rich Pickings in Asian Shipping Lanes', *The Guardian*, 2 February 2001.

[54] Yeoh En-lai, 'Pirate Attacks in Region on the Rise', *Straits Times*, 5 November 2000.

[55] 'Piracy in South-east Asia: Obstacles to Security Cooperation'; Solomon Kane and Laurent Passicousset, 'Pirates of the South China Sea', *Le Monde Diplomatique*, June 2000.

[56] 'No Anti-Piracy Patrols in South-east Asia', *Asian Defence Journal*, 7/2001, p. 43.

[57] 'Singapore and Japan To Step Up Dialogue Interactions and Exchanges', Singapore Ministry of Defence website, 2 May 2000, www.mindef.gov.sg

[58] Kwan Weng Kin, 'Asian Governments Not Keen on

Joint Piracy Patrols', *Straits Times*, 4 May 2000; 'Piracy in South-east Asia: Obstacles to Security Cooperation'; 'Japan To Hold Joint Piracy Drills', *ibid.*, 21 October 2000.

59 'South Korea and Indonesia Hold Second Naval Meeting', *Yonhap* news agency, 2 February 1999, in SWB/FE/3450 D/3, 4 February 1999.

60 'Navy Reveals Plan To Fight Piracy', *Jakarta Post*, 5 November 2000.

61 'Naval Commander Replaced After Recent Piracy Outbreak', *Media Indonesia*, 29 March 2001, in SWB/FE/4108 B/2, 30 March 2001.

62 Reme Ahmad, 'Pirates Raid Third Ship Off Indonesia', *Straits Times*, 28 June 2001.

63 Yeoh En-lai, 'Indonesia's Anti-Piracy Centre Gets Lukewarm Response', *ibid.*, 27 October 2001.

64 'Naval Spending To Increase in Light of Policy Shift', *Radio Australia*, 25 October 1999, in SWB/FE/3675 B/4, 26 October 1999; Kurniawan Hari, 'Low Funds Hamper Navy: Official', *Jakarta Post*, 8 October 2001.

65 'Piracy Watchdog Points Finger at Aceh Separatists', *Straits Times*, 4 February 2002.

66 'Malaysia Steps Up Patrols in Straits After Threats from Rebel Acehnese', *Jakarta Post*, 6 September 2001.

67 'US Escorts Key Supply Ships through Malacca Strait', *Straits Times*, 4 December 2001.

68 Nirmal Ghosh, 'India's Navy Joins US War on Terrorism', *Straits Times*, 24 April 2002.

69 Alan Dupont, *East Asia Imperilled: Transnational Challenges to Security* (Cambridge: Cambridge University Press, 2001), pp. 53–55.

70 Devi Asmarani, 'Stricter Laws To Stop Forest Fires', *Straits Times*, 28 February 2001.

71 Dupont, *East Asia Imperilled*, p. 55.

72 Asmarani, 'Stricter Laws'.

73 Marianne Kearney, 'Déjà Vu in Riau as Haze Returns', *Straits Times*, 16 March 2002.

74 Dupont, *East Asia Imperilled*, p. 58.

75 *East Asian Strategic Review 2001* (Tokyo: National Institute for Defense Studies, 2001), p. 85.

76 'Wolfowitz Interview with Asian Wall Street Journal', US Department of Defense News Transcript, 27 March 2002, *DefenseLINK* website, www.defenselink.mil

77 Derwin Pereira, 'Region's Forces Can Play Wider Role in Indonesia', *Straits Times*, 14 August 2000.

78 Peter Lewis Young, 'Australia–Indonesia Relations – Never the Same Again?', *Asian Defence Journal*, 9/2000, p. 7.